THE STEPMOMS' CLUB

D0468792

THE

Stepmoms'

CLUB

*How to Be a Stepmom without Losing
Your Money, Your Mind, and Your Marriage*

KENDALL ROSE

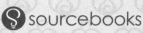

Published by Sourcebooks, Inc.
P.O. Box 4410, Naperville, Illinois 60567-4410
(630) 961-3900
Fax: (630) 961-2168
sourcebooks.com

Library of Congress Cataloging-in-Publication Data

Names: Rose, Kendall, author.
Title: The stepmoms' club : how to be a stepmom without losing your money,
   your mind, and your marriage / Kendall Rose.
Description: Naperville : Sourcebooks, Inc., [2018]
Identifiers: LCCN 2017051757 | (pbk. : alk. paper)
Subjects: LCSH: Stepmothers. | Stepmothers--Family relationships. |
   Self-actualization (Psychology)
Classification: LCC HQ759.92 .R667 2018 | DDC 306.874/7--dc23 LC record avail-
able at https://lccn.loc.gov/2017051757

Printed and bound in the United States of America.
VP 10 9 8 7 6 5 4 3 2 1

Table of Contents

Introduction

DEAR STEPMOM OR STEPMOM-TO-BE,

Happy Mother's Day.

There. We needed to get that out of the way, no matter what day it is, even if it's not Mother's Day. It's important you hear Happy Mother's Day, because if you're a stepmom, chances are you don't hear it. Whether you're a newbie stepmom or an in-the-trenches, dozen year career stepmom, chances are that Mother's Day comes and goes with no acknowledgment of your role of *mother*. Sure, you may not be a mother in the *biological* sense, but you are in a way that counts, in the way that you drive five hours round-trip to soccer matches, wipe bloody noses, make lunches and dinners, and stand in for the tooth fairy and Santa.

You're doing mothering duties (or you're about to take them on), and yet you're relegated to the title held by some of the most evil characters in fairy-tale history. It's archaic and unfair casting, and unless you are a stepmom, you cannot fully understand what being a stepmom means and, more importantly, what it feels like.

No one sees the *shit* behind the stepmom curtain better than other stepmoms—the dozens of women we interviewed and whose stories we included in this book will attest to that.

We're going to help you be a stepmom, no matter whether you've been at this stepmothering business longer than you care to recall or you're first starting to dip your toes into some shark-infested step waters. That's what this book is all about. We've got your back, because we've been there, we *are* there, and we're in it for the whole ride. We're lifers, all of us, and if you'll let us, we will give you not only the plain-and-simple facts of stepmothering, but the messy, complicated, rewarding, heartrending, and heartwarming insights gained through what we've lived and learned as stepmoms.

Who Are We?

We are Kendall, Elizabeth, Stephanie, and Amber—stepmoms, all of us. Collectively, we are the Stepmoms' Club, to which we welcome *you*! Since this book was a joint endeavor between the four of us—a labor of love, really—we'll be referring to ourselves along the way as "we." *We* want to impart the advice (and warnings) we desperately wished we'd been given before we became stepmoms, advice that we couldn't find in volume after volume of "helpful" clinical wisdom by therapists and PhDs. You know the kinds of books we mean: *How to Blend Your New Family* (yeah, slowly, with lots of ice and tequila would have been a more helpful recipe than the ones we read), *How to Get the Respect You Deserve* (sounds like a manual for middle management), and *How to Set Boundaries* (which are bound to be broken and reset unless you're Vladimir Putin).

Please note that for the purpose of consistency, and because we all married *men* with children, we may refer to the spouse or partner as "husband," but as we've learned, with the rise of same-sex marriages, the statistics for lesbian divorce are fast approaching those of straight couples. So, ladies, if your spouse or prospective spouse, partner, boyfriend, or girlfriend has kids, welcome to the club, too!

At this point, chances are you already *are* a stepmom and you're thinking, *I had no idea what I was signing up for as a stepmom!* Or you're soon to be a stepmom and you're wondering, *How hard could it possibly be?* (Cue the laugh track.) So let's start with some statistics. Approximately fifty percent of first marriages end in divorce (that percentage is 67 to 80 for second marriages),* so chances are high that a divorced adult will remarry someone with kids. An estimated one-third of American children will live in a stepparent family before the age of eighteen, and 50 percent of children will have a stepparent at some point in their lifetime. According to the U.S.

---

* Health Research Funding, March 20, 2015, http://healthresearchfunding. org/55-surprising-divorce-statistics-second-marriages/.

Census Bureau, half of the sixty million American children under the age of thirteen are currently living with *one* biological parent and that parent's current partner. In the United States alone, there are fifteen million stepmoms! With numbers like these, you might wonder where the support groups are for stepmoms. We couldn't find them—how strange. There are support groups for single moms and single parents, fathers, teens, families, adoptees, and mothers, so how is it that there hasn't been one for stepmoms…until now?

We're right here. We are a support group for any woman finding herself in the role of stepmom—whether you're the stepmom-by-proxy partner, the fiancée stepmom-to-be, or a stepmom via marriage—because we realized early on that *we* needed *our own* group. There are millions of us, from every race, religion, color, and socioeconomic status. We are nonexclusive, to be sure—an equal opportunity society that no one ever sets out to be part of. Yet here we are.

Truly, who else but another stepmom is going to understand what it is to *be a stepmom*? Who else but a fellow stepmom will understand when you need to bitch about a crazy ex and her impossible demands? Who else will understand the elation of a first amiable dinner with the stepkids or the first time your stepson invites you to his ballgame *without* paternal prompts? Who else is going to understand how humbling/frustrating/mind-blowing it is to be a stepmom?

Three of us four stepmoms have known each other for more than twenty years. We met the fourth in our group when our biological (bio) kids started preschool. Right off the bat, we bonded over our roles as stepmoms. It was as if we'd found our people, our *tribe*. We soon graduated to a monthly girls' night out in order to finish conversations we started on the playground. We talked. And talked. And talked…about our partners, children, bosses, parents, and in-laws—all the things that women talk about when said partners, children, bosses, parents, and in-laws aren't around. It wasn't long before we realized that we all dwelled on one pressing, common topic—being a stepmom—and how and why *no one* prepared us for that role. How was it, we wondered, that no alarms blared, no caution lights blazed, not one damn friend, acquaintance, or family member stepped forward to raise a red flag and proclaim, "Wait a freakin' moment and take stock of what you're getting yourself into!" Why did no one tell us that in real life the role of a stepmom is a helluva lot more like that of Cinderella—before the happy ending—than it is like Lady Tremaine, Cinderella's wicked stepmother. If you are a stepmom, you know we kid you not.

That reminds us. We in no way care to dis our dear, nonstepmom friends, of which we have many. They are some of the smartest, well-intentioned people we know. In fact, their advice certainly is welcome (when we ask for it) and valued, because oftentimes, they are able to see the forest for the trees, if only because they don't live in our particular *stepmom* forest. A good friend of ours who happens to be an attorney is always quick to point out, "Why do you even give a f*** about [insert crazy ex, stepkid, or infuriating situation here]?" Occasionally, she'll give us pause, but more often than not, we respond with, "You can't understand because you're not a stepmom."

"It can't be that bad," she'll counter.

If she only knew.

It's doubtful that any woman, when imagining a future life of marriage and kids, pictures herself as a stepmom. Imagine the proverbial fairy-tale princess welcoming her knight in shining armor on a white steed, except that he's pulling a bulging carriage (more like a circus clown car) filled with children, an ex, and assorted former in-laws. As a kid, do you remember any girlfriends who ever mused over Legos or tea parties, "I can't wait until I grow up and become a stepmom!" (Keep in mind that it's equally doubtful that any child would choose to be a step*child*.) It's a scenario that doesn't figure into anyone's dream goal.

In fact, a Boston University psychologist and researcher reported that of the career women who earned more than $100,000 and had married men with children, over 75 percent reported that if they had it to do again, they would *not* marry a man with children.*

---

*   "Stepfamily Statistics," The Step Family Foundation, accessed September 25, 2017, www.stepfamily.org/stepfamily-statistics.html.

Hear what we just said: 75 percent of women who had married men with children said that they *would not* do it again. Ever. Again. Period. Hindsight is a beautiful thing, isn't it? And we're here to tell you that it is okay to feel that way, because there are days when you *will* feel that way if you haven't already. Fortunately, though, through trial and error, trauma and tears and wisdom earned, *we* are happy to report that we would do it again—well, most likely, anyway.

We are four independent women with careers and goals, friends and family, and we have between us four husbands, five ex-wives, five bio children, and eight stepchildren. Over the years, we've invited to our stepmom round table a new stepmom or two, someone in our extended circle who needed support or, alternately, someone who was open to giving us the advice or assurance *we* needed. There were times our group was so big, it was like a postbachelorette party that had fallen down some stepmothering rabbit hole—including step friends of step friends, park acquaintance steps, fellow soccer and ballet steps, Lamaze and long-distance steps. We listened (and learned) from one another's stories, and we offered each other suggestions (sometimes taken, sometimes ignored until a later moment of desperation). We acknowledged our fears, and we allowed ourselves admissions of feeling differently about our stepchildren than our bio kids.

At our get-togethers, we confessed to hiding in bedrooms and basements when the stepkids came over, we sobbed after failed stepfamily weekends, and then we hammered out ways to find small, ordinary successes, if only for an afternoon. We commiserated about ex-wives who used threatening measures—restraining orders, vicious emails and calls—and teenage tactics such as evil glares over a soccer field or across a recital room. Sticks and stones may break bones, ladies, but glares will be ignored and laughed about later with step friends.

We realized that in order to fully understand how impossible, infuriating, unappreciated, and thankless the role of stepmom can be, one would have to *be* a stepmom. At the same time, only we stepmoms could fully appreciate the rewards and joy of hard-won successes and small, unsolicited kindnesses. We could hardly wait for our monthly meetings, especially if there was a particular dilemma at hand. Come on, would you trust a book about childrearing to someone who has never reared a child, a book on success in advertising to someone who has never run a successful ad campaign? So it came to be that we made ourselves available to each other by phone and text 24/7. Sometimes support means listening to a sobbing, frustrated stepmom friend at 2:00 a.m. after she's heard her stepdaughter's misery-laden plea to her dad, "What could you possibly see in *her*?" Lifelines are not lifelines if they're only available once a month during happy hour.

As in an excellent adult education or postgraduate course taught by someone in the field, we *learned*. We learned from each other how to connect to the issues at hand, and, in many cases, how to *let go*. Together, we took baby steps, amended goals, changed old beliefs and attitudes, and helped each other to maintain sanity. Most of all, we realized we were on a journey that would prove to be ongoing and ever shifting, one that required assistance and at least a few second mates.

A couple of years ago, at one of our monthly gatherings, we turned over a place mat and made a list of everything we wish we knew *before* we said "I do." Several hours and a dozen place mats later, we realized we could fill a book, and then we proceeded to do so. In the making of this book, we hoped to reach out to the woman who is not only in the throes of a marriage with a partner who came with kids, but also the woman who is contemplating such a marriage, because, well, forewarned is forearmed. Our aim is to give you a tactical advantage in your role as stepmom by offering various scenarios and solutions.

Some of our stepmom stories may seem the worst experiences of what stepmothering can be. However, we're certain there are even worse out there, somewhere (frighteningly enough), and the reason for our presenting them is that we and our fellow stepmoms eventually found some sort of resolution in the chaos. Ultimately, that's really all we're looking for: some kind of resolution in our relationships with our stepkids, our partners, and even the bio mothers of our stepkids.

Our one disclaimer might be: if you're having a wonderful relationship with your partner's ex—she's "like" your BFF—or your stepfamily life would put the Brady Bunch to shame, then this book is not for you. We're just trying to save you some time here. (If, indeed, you are the stepmom who has avoided struggle and strife and has never for a nanosecond fathomed running away from home, we would be very curious to hear what prescription drugs you might be taking.)

If you're still wondering if this book is for *you*, you may want to ask yourself the following questions:

- Am I a priority in my partner's life? Is he/she committed to our relationship first and foremost?
- Is the mother of my partner's kid(s) insane? Is she manipulative?
- Does my new partner ever say no to the ex? Better yet, does my new partner feel so guilty about his divorce that he will let his ex control every aspect of his kids' lives (thereby controlling *my* life)?
- Will the ex's meddling family now be involved in my life as well?
- Is my new partner the stereotypical Disneyland dad (or mom) when the kids are with us?
- Is my partner responsible for the kind of child

support and/or alimony payments that would put
a burden on our lifestyle together?

- Will I be part of the collateral damage caused by
  my partner's children or ex?

If these questions give you pause about dating or marrying someone with kids, this book is for you.

If you're deep into dating or marriage to someone with kids and you've asked yourself none of the aforementioned questions but wish you had, this book is for you.

If you had the wherewithal to ask yourself all those questions and you ignored your own less-than-satisfactory answers, and especially if you believe that romantic love conquers all and these questions are irrelevant, then this book is definitely for you.

So, dear stepmom, if you are hoping to recognize what is already in your life and gain some practical, tried, and tested solutions, or if you're simply at the point of *considering* getting involved with someone who has kids, then please read on. Whether you're married, living with your partner, dating, fantasizing a life with a partner who has kids, or hoping to understand a beloved stepmom in your life a little better, we are certain you'll benefit from these things we wish we knew before we said "I do."

Welcome to the club.

CHAPTER 1

What Am I Getting Myself Into?

IN THE SPIRIT OF HOPE, WE WILL SAY THAT WITH TIME comes wisdom. If you're a newbie stepmom, you may be feeling a little as you did when you were a college (or high school) freshman, in that you're all starry-eyed and enthusiastic about your new or soon-to-be role. You may have high expectations for this next chapter of your life, along with plans to create the perfect stepfamily. And that's an admirable thing, but as battle-weary stepmoms, we're more like fifth-year, wiser-for-wear college seniors who have the experience and knowledge gained from overstaying an education. Sure, we can still summon a certain amount of enthusiasm and goodwill, but we've learned, above everything else, to have no expectations.

As much as we plan to address both newbie stepmoms and women who have been in the step trenches for years, this particular first chapter seems best suited for that rising-freshman stepmom. Consider it an advance look at your upcoming stepmom education. That's not to say you career stepmoms and those of you who may already have had the stars knocked out of your eyes will not find some interesting pointers in here, especially when it comes to making sure that your partner has removed his ex's name from all important financial documents—more on that later in this chapter. But first, a few pointers.

Read Your Partner's Divorce Decree and Custody Agreement

"What?" you may be asking yourself. "I have to do *what*? *When*? *Why*?"

Okay, we'll back up a little and ease into this first step. Let's imagine you've already said "I do," or you're two minutes away from uttering those two little words, or you're contemplating marriage or cohabitation to someone with kids, or you're in a relationship with a parent and it feels like it's progressing toward something more exclusive. If any of those situations applies to you, then we ask you to heed this first chapter of advice: give the divorce decree and custody agreement a good read. Trust us, this first step is important.

You're only "DATING"—notice all caps—you may argue. But if you've gotten far enough in the relationship where you're picking up a potential stepkid from school (or her mother's, or piano lessons, or soccer practice) in a pinch, it's not a bad time to look into that decree and custody crystal ball and see what *may* be in your future. You may even be able to help your boy/girlfriend deal with a frustrating or difficult situation by providing a relatively unbiased eye. Yes, we know, you're only *dating*. Got it. But please understand, in that wonderful place of hindsight, most of us wish we'd read the documents far earlier. Read them.

> "I was sitting on the couch in my living room when my fiancé handed me a folder and said to me, 'Uh, I think it would be a good idea if you read this.' Love poems? Short stories from his college days? I opened the folder and took out his divorce agreement. I think I would have been less scared had it been a zombie apocalypse movie. Quite frankly, I had second thoughts on the marriage for the next few days." —August

We understand that if you're in the throes of planning your dream wedding, it might feel very unromantic to bring up the ex and those pesky agreements. Can't it wait for another time, you ask? After all, the wedding is not about *her*. Well, we beg to differ, especially if the ex is rigid about whose week(end) is whose with regard to custody of the kids.

Take this one example: let's say you've got a small enough window for the wedding as it is, what with all your and your intended's work and family schedules. You've figured in his vacation time and yours, and when your parents will be back from their fortieth wedding anniversary trip, and when your preferred venue will be available. Now you're reading his divorce papers and realizing you have to get married on "his" weekend, meaning that in order for his kids to attend (which, of course, you both want to happen), you've got to figure *that* variable into the equation. And wait, the week you're planning as your honeymoon isn't *her* week—and truth be told, the only reason the ex will consider rearranging the custody schedule is in the case of a funeral (his or yours, perhaps).

For many stepmoms (a couple of us included), 90 percent of arguments between couples are about the ex and the custody and visitation arrangements. So if you're planning a wedding, honeymoon, or other family-centric event (or an event that specifically *doesn't* include your partner's kids), don't start with a request to change the edicts of the custody agreement and the weekend schedule, unless there is no way humanly possible to change your own plans. It's not worth the argument, and certainly, it's not worth a trip to the lawyers' office, unless you don't mind putting the money for your dream Belize honeymoon into an attorney's retirement account. Read the papers and plan accordingly!

Honeymoon not in the stars anyway, you say—and besides, you're totally flexible because the only trip in your budget right now is a weekend at the Jersey Shore. Well, what about a baby?

Yours. The one you might have with your new partner. Yeah, *that* baby. We'll call her Future Baby. What happens when Future Baby comes into the world on "his" weekend with the kids? Or let's say his kids are psyched for Future Baby and want to be there for the arrival of their newest sib, but the ex doesn't want to deviate from the custody agreement. What then? You may be laughing, because you're thinking, *Now who in their right mind wouldn't amend a schedule in order to accommodate a birth, for God's sake?* And therein lies our point. The motto of scouting (and stepmothering): Be Prepared. *Be prepared.* (We'll be driving this one home a lot along the way.)

For those of you who are already married, it's not too late to read the decree and agreement. We urge you to do so. Now.

"As I read my husband's decree, I realized that there were a lot of 'gray areas' that left way too much to interpretation, which, in my husband's case, meant that he was allowing his ex-wife to make decisions that he ought to have been consulted on, such as which doctors and dentists their kids should see. Birthday celebrations were supposed to be decided mutually and shared together, but in reality, my husband and his ex wound up having separate celebrations, which were like competitions with invitees feeling that they had to choose which party to attend. But, I thought, those were his problems, not mine. Big mistake, because I soon realized that in marrying my husband, I had essentially married his ex-wife, too. I had no idea that between sporting events, dance recitals, school functions, and day-to-day pickups and drop-offs, I'd be seeing his ex five times a week… or more! As much as my mood was often dampened by these interactions, my husband's mood was blackened in dealing with his ex. Since they were so mutually disdainful of each other, his whole demeanor would change after seeing her, so much so that he'd lash out at me! I finally put my foot down and told him that I wasn't his ex and that his anxiety was about her, not us. I told him that it was time to get professional help—actually, I insisted. To his credit, he did, and it made a world of difference in our marriage." —Daniella

Every detail of your partner's financial responsibility is, most likely, in his divorce decree and custody agreement—from alimony to child support, school tuition to piano lessons, allergist visits to soccer camp—along with his parental obligations. The weekly visits, alternate holidays, summer vacations are in there as well. For those of you who have already made the proverbial leap, reading these legal documents may help you to better understand the variables that have been driving you crazy.

That said, the frustrating thing is that no matter how specifically an agreement is worded, there still may be room for interpretation. A good example of this is when a weekend begins. Does it *begin* at 4:00 p.m. Friday, at the end of the school day, or maybe it means an early Saturday wake-up call because Friday night is technically part of the workweek. Or is it? Who says? Do violin lessons mean the long-standing bargain lessons with a student teacher, or can the ex abruptly decide that junior is a budding concert musician who requires lessons with a member of the New York Philharmonic?

"On the surface, my husband's custody and visitation agreement seemed very black and white, but it turned out to have more than fifty shades of gray. The papers said that we'd have his kids every other weekend and every other school break for a three- or four-day holiday. Unfortunately, there was a difference of opinion as to when a weekend or holiday began and ended. His ex-wife insisted that his visitation started with school's end at 3:10 (sharp) on Fridays. Well, we both worked, so we couldn't pick the kids up until 6:00 p.m. at their mother's home. She also insisted that the kids be dropped off at her house by 1:00 p.m. on Sundays so they had plenty of time to do their homework in their 'own environment'—as if my husband and I lived in some foreign and hostile suburban land. Despite the aggravation of keeping with these rules, and despite our civilized attempts at reason, my husband's ex considered them to be nonnegotiable. Eventually, costly lawyers had to be brought in to negotiate a compromise as simple as our picking the kids up between 6:00 and 6:30 on Fridays and returning them to their mom's house at 5:00 p.m. on Sunday. What a waste of time, money, and emotions it was to bring in lawyers. But what I learned was that every single detail regarding custody and visitation needs to be spelled out to avoid miscommunication and email wars." —Kendall

Be aware that as you're reading the terms and responsibilities of your partner's divorce decree and custody plan, you may be tempted to call out, "Oh my God, pour me a scotch, honey. And by the way, what the hell were you thinking when you agreed to all this?" We'd like to advise you *not* to go the offensive route here, as it helps no one, especially you and your partner or soon-to-be-spouse. Bear in mind that emotions may have been especially heated when your partner and his ex were hammering out the decree and custody agreement. In hindsight, he may be thinking to himself, "Oh God, what did I agree to?" and "Please don't punish me for whatever cockamamie reason it was." Take a breath and try to imagine (and take into account) his emotional state during all the final decision making.

Look, you fell in love, and you want the marriage to work, so you have to remain positive. By reading all the legal stuff, you will at least have some awareness of his responsibilities and yours. Talk through what you don't understand or what seems unclear. If you're well informed, you can make informed choices—one of which may be to marry the guy anyway and try to create the loving home you've always imagined. On the other hand, if the divorce and custody terms read like some Gothic romance novel gone tragically wrong, then it may be time to think twice. If anything, at least discuss your fear or trepidation. It's a great excuse to start setting up those lines of candid communication. There'll be no misunderstanding that your partner "forgot" to tell you about the extra $750 a month he promised to shell out for art, music, swimming, dancing, gymnastics, and fencing lessons, and that (oops) he has no say in choice or location of said lessons, so you're stuck driving his little darling an hour each way in order to appease everyone involved.

The Money Issues

Is he shelling out the money for "extras" and tutoring and insurance even though his ex is the one allowed, as per the divorce terms, to claim the kids on *her* tax return? Is there an annual cost of living increase built into the agreements even though he's in a job or career that doesn't keep up with the national norm? Does the agreement state that your partner is obligated to continue paying the ex's health and auto insurance? If so, for how long? Will orthodontic braces or college expenses be split? If that seems too far away, then what about day care and private school? What constitutes an "extraordinary expense"?

Look closely, as there may also be milestones in the agreement, corresponding to an end in support or certain financial responsibilities. If you insist that the money issues are "his thing," you might want to ask yourself how it will impact your new household and what financial sacrifices you may have to make.

The Time Issues

Your time. What is your time worth, and more importantly, how much of your time are you willing to sacrifice?

If his kids are sick and must stay home for the day, who looks after them, Mom or Dad? If it's Dad but he can't afford to miss a workday, can you? If your partner is responsible, then that means *you* are now responsible (remember the prince's carriage in your driveway?), and if you do wind up being the designated nurse more times than you'd imagined, are you going to start seething in resentment? What about snow days, school half days, three-day weekends, and business trips? Rules can run the gamut from indecipherable gray areas to control-freak specific.

The Authority Issues

Who has the authority in regard to your stepkids' health? In regard to illness—or checkups or those pesky school registration forms that require a doctor's visit and extensive Q & A—you'll need to know which parent, if not both, has authority to choose a pediatrician. Has the ex chosen someone who is thirty miles and an hour and a half out of town, and little Jeremy needs weekly allergy shots? Are *both* parents listed as emergency contacts?

It's a slippery slope that can result in embarrassing situations like your stepdaughter ending up in the hospital with a broken arm and the ex just happening to forget to list the father as an emergency contact, or worse, as a member of the immediate family. Dad winds up at the nurse's station trying to convince a harried staff that he's allowed to see his own kid. As the partner, are you on the emergency contact list (as opposed to the grandparent who lives out of state and certainly can't be of immediate help from fifteen hundred miles away)?

"My husband would pick up his daughter every Wednesday evening for dinner from her after-school program. The custody agreement stated that the teacher had to call the ex-wife when he arrived so that she could give permission to the teacher for my husband's daughter to leave with him. Every Wednesday, it was the same deal. It was like he was under house arrest and his parole officer was giving him license to be with his own daughter. I swear, I think she put that clause in the papers just to try and humil-iate him. We had to go back to court to change that stupid stipulation." —Beatrice

It's not just schedules and demands revolving around the kids that can drive a stepmom mad. Sometimes a furry family member can threaten to turn even the most devout pet lover into a woman with a pet death wish. File under pets are family, too.

"I almost choked when I read my husband's divorce papers. His ex included six pages of detailed notes about the shared care and custody of their cat, Mimi (in contrast to the three pages regarding custody matters for their son). Mimi could only see 'her' vet (on the ex's side of town). The dimensions of her litter box and carrier, the brand of kitty litter she could tolerate, and the high-end cat food she needed were all nonnegotiable. Even though cats are known for their ability to be on their own as long as they have food and water, Mimi, sensitive as she was, could not be left home alone for more than twenty-four hours. If my husband and I were going out of town for longer than a day, we had to notify the ex so she could take her. Mimi was allowed to spend every other week and alternate Christmas and Easter vacations with us. After five years of joint custody and several heated arguments with the ex over perceived transgressions of the rules, Mimi died at the ripe old age of 17 (that's 119 in human years—we should all live so long). In hindsight, my husband and I realized that his ex's 'Mimi rants' weren't about anything other than her wanting to maintain some control of his (and our) life. Even so..." —Amber

---

If you've read the court papers and you're naive enough to think that you'll be able to change what doesn't make sense to you, then read them again with the understanding that ninety-nine times out of a hundred, no amount of arguing is going to change what's in those papers. Once you understand your partner's responsibilities, financial and custody, you can begin to

accept and let go. Breathe in. Breathe out. If that doesn't work and
you absolutely feel the need to vent your anger and disbelief—*I
mean, how crazy/stupid/desperate does someone have to be to agree to
[fill in the blank]*—save it. Call a friend. Better yet, call a stepmom
(more on this later).

"When I read my husband Tim's divorce decree, everything seemed fine. He and his ex, 'Louise,' had joint
legal custody—which means that they shared the
decision-making responsibilities and custody of their
son—except when it came to religious decisions, which
were her call. Before Tim and I married, we purchased
a house and lived together with my two children from
my previous marriage. For financial reasons, I wanted
to remain 'head of household,' so we chose not to
marry. As a born-again Christian (when it suited her),
Louise pulled out the religion card and wouldn't allow
their son to spend even one night in our 'House of Sin.'
Tim and I spoke to a mediator who said he had never
read anything like this before and suggested returning to court. Well, we did the math on what that would
cost, so rather than throwing away time and money
with lawyers and the court system, we got married."
—Elizabeth

No Ex in Sight?

A young woman one of us knows recently started dating a guy who has custody of his four-year-old. We nearly fell over ourselves in asking, "Where is the ex? Is she alive?" (No, sometimes we're not as subtle as we would like to be.) Why the surprise, you ask?

Here's the issue: despite our day and age of equal rights, parental and otherwise, it's usually a huge deal for the mother not to have at least partial custody of her child(ren) in the case of divorce. If you're involved with someone who has full custody of his or her child, and the mother is, indeed, still alive, you need to find out why the ex did not receive custody. Did she not want it? Where is she? Is she in a hospital (mental or otherwise)? Is she alcoholic, a chronic drug user, an inmate in a women's penitentiary? Then you, yourself, must understand that if she does have some kind of a problem but works her way toward functional, she may then want to be a part of her child's life after all. No matter what the circumstances (sobriety, recovery, or whatever), they may change, in which case the bio mom may want to come back into the picture.

It may seem difficult to understand why a child's own mother would not be a part of that child's life, but you can't know the whole story unless you ask: Where is the mom? Find out.

Accept and Respect What Is

Consider yourself lucky if your partner's ex is flexible when it comes to changing the previously arranged pickup and drop-off times and weekend and vacation custody arrangements. But if your partner tells you (or you've found out the hard way) that his ex goes nuclear at the slightest change in plans, chances are that there are control issues at play, and you will not win at making changes, no matter your reasoning.

A change of plans may be necessary in an emergency—a real emergency, like bleeding from the head or a zombie apocalypse. Otherwise, stick to the court-ordered agreement. If, after time and changes in circumstances, you and your partner find that it's necessary to modify the existing agreement, then your partner and his ex will probably find themselves back in court, in which case the following will be considered: the child's well-being and her relationship with her parents, the child's wishes, and maybe even the conduct of the parents. You'll need to check your state's laws and standards to find out what you and your partner can and cannot legally do in terms of changing existing agreements.

For now, leave yourself plenty of time if you're picking the kids up or dropping them off at the ex's house. Even an excuse as benign as "the traffic was horrendous" can sound like a manipulative play and wind up igniting issues that have nothing to do with you or your traffic karma. If being late is beyond your control, then text or call. Make it short and sweet, and by all means, be courteous, even if she's not.

She Is Not

Let's say that you and your partner are trying your damnedest to be polite, given that you're also trying to deal with the rest of what's on your plate—multiple jobs, other children, money woes, pets, whatever—while the ex is being purposely disruptive. So what happens when the ex's passive-aggressive lateness and "time mismanagement" starts taking a toll on your new nuclear family? If court is out of the question, what can you do?

This is a tough one, for sure, and it comes up time and time again. You, the stepmom, probably feel like the bio mom gets away with everything and that she's the one who never has to give in. For your own sanity and sense of control (however useless or false it may seem in the end), you must document everything. Hear us? Document, document, document. Save the emails, the texts, and the letters…everything. Write down the crazy conversations—the time and date and place. This is for you, and it *may* come in handy if, in the extreme circumstance, you do wind up going to court.

On the other hand, your documentation may merely be a useful exercise in maintaining your sanity, because in the end, you may have to finally accept that there isn't a whole hell of a lot that you can change. Court dates can be made and broken and under-scored in screaming matches and lost time, in which case you may wish that you'd never brought up the idea of a court-mandated solution. The ending to this story, the answer to "But what do I do?" is this: accept that you won't change much in court-mandated agreements. The sooner you accept this fact, the better off you'll be—emotionally and physically. Seriously.

"It's so aggravating when you and your husband stick to the schedule, but the ex doesn't. My husband and I made every effort to be prompt when dropping off or picking up his kids. If we were going to be late, we called. My stepchildren's mother was supposed to drop the kids off at our house on Friday evenings at let's say 7:00 p.m., but many times, she was an hour or two late, which often reduced my young daughter, Hannah, to tears, because she looked forward to seeing her brother and sister. Our solution was that instead of telling Hannah what time her siblings would arrive, my husband and I instead promised her that she would see them sometime before bedtime, which at least eliminated the waiting game. We'd go along with our usual Friday night routine with less expectation, and in fact, Hannah was glad just to say hello and good night. When the kids arrived late, they were often cranky, tired, and hungry, and we were prepared for that as well. My guess is that the ex did this to gain some sort of control over all of us—the truth being that it was her kids who suffered. By knowing what to expect, we mostly avoided big blowups." —Kendall

---

When (not *if*) you find yourself upset at something the ex has done, you may, understandably, think your partner is equally upset. Here's a news flash: that won't necessarily be the case. There's a good chance that your partner will be far less upset at the things that are upsetting you, maybe because he's already sweated such big and emotionally charged issues with his ex, or maybe because he's too racked with guilt—over the failure of his marriage, the toll of divorce on his kids, or the fact that he's moved on while his ex hasn't—to sweat the small stuff this time around. In that case, you need to ask yourself whether the things you're upset about are really worth your mental agitation.

"Sometimes it's up to you, the stepmom, to know what the particulars are in the decree, to step in and take the reins, because otherwise, the ex will constantly push the envelope. Seriously, save yourself some aggravation.

Stated in my partner's decree was that on the Thursdays his son was with us, he would take over at 6:00 p.m. This was written in the decree...6:00 p.m., despite the fact that my stepson got out of school at 2:45 p.m. So, because the ex didn't work, she was responsible for making arrangements until 6:00. Instead, every other week or so, the ex would text my partner at the last minute and say, 'Hey, you have to pick up your son.' He would scramble to find a way to get him because he didn't want to deal with his ex-wife going into a tizzy. After perusing the decree and seeing how stressed my partner got, I thought, this has to stop. I told him to preempt the text nonsense, in writing, first thing in the morning with a text of his own saying, 'Remember, I work until 6:00, so you must pick up Kevin.' Period. Oftentimes, it will be up to you to provide a solution...or clarity." —Marissa

---

Your initial road map for how to navigate financial responsibility and scheduling is in the decree. Even if you feel at some point that you've read enough, keep reading. Get all your WTF moments out in one fell swoop. By the end of your little research session, you'll be familiar not only with your partner's custody schedule and financial obligations, but you'll also have a better understanding of what responsibilities you may be sharing with your partner.

Beyond the Decree: Financial Management

In the spirit of being proactive about your partner's financial situation, you might want to confirm with your partner that his ex's name is off all his bank and credit card accounts and is removed as beneficiary in any life insurance and pension policies (unless he is legally required to keep his ex on the policy, per the divorce agreement.). That advice bears repeating, because even if you are married to your partner, if the ex is not off the life insurance and pension policies, you will be facing a legal nightmare in the case of unforeseen and tragic circumstances.

Life insurance and pension are the big, obvious policies, but what about the accounts that haven't been in play for a while, like department store accounts, equity credit lines, brokerage accounts, or safe-deposit boxes? If your partner has his grandma's Tiffany ring along with the deed to a small tract of land in Wyoming that he's set aside for retirement in a forgotten safe-deposit box (jointly owned with the ex), then, quite literally, whoever grabs those things first is the keeper of said things. If that box is cleared out, there's little chance of recovering any of the contents, even if their worth is only of sentimental value (with any luck, all that's left in that joint safe-deposit box will be Grandpa's dentures). Alternately, ask your partner to make certain that he is taken off his ex's policies and accounts!

Just to hit you over the head with gusto: once you've confirmed that your partner *thinks* he's taken care of changing over financial matters such as the automatic bank and credit card billing, double-check. Make sure the bills that aren't his responsibility haven't "magically"—excuse us for our lack of postdivorce financial faith—remained routed to his accounts and been paid without his knowledge.

"Sounds more urban divorce legend than not, but this happened to my best friend from college. Manny was in his early forties when he remarried after a horrible knock-down-drag-out divorce. His ex-wife had crazy, unrealistic money demands, which Manny met because she used their kids as pawns and hired outrageously expensive lawyers. Finally, the smoke cleared, and after a couple of years, Manny and his new wife had a baby. He's happy, and his kids from his first marriage are even happy. Happy ending, right? Manny goes out on his morning jog, has a massive heart attack, and dies. Horrible. His wife weeds through the will and all his accounts (yes, he did at least change the will) and discovers that although he'd updated all the medical information and insurance documents, he had forgotten to take the ex off as beneficiary for his 401K, so the ex, not his kids from his previous marriage and not his widow, walked away with all the money. His company felt awful, but there wasn't a thing they could legally do to counteract that one accounting oversight. It still makes me mad!" —Wendy

---

The point we're trying to bring home is: educate yourself as much as possible, and ask as many questions as need be. Also, murmur as few WTFs as possible, aloud or under your breath. Think of the process we have outlined in chapter one as research for the itinerary of your new life. There are stops you have to make, places you have to be, and times to be there, but don't worry. There'll be detours aplenty and, with effort, some wonderful things to see.

Whether you've skipped to the end of this first chapter or read through it and inked the margins with copious "notes to self," we've briefly highlighted what we think are the most important takeaways.

TAKEAWAYS

- Read your partner's divorce decree and custody agreement immediately. Now. Knowing what's in those papers will help to avoid arguments with your partner about money, custody, holidays, drop-offs, pickups, etc.

- Have your partner show you a road map of the money, where it's going and for how long.
- Understand what your role as stepmom is expected to be.
- Know who has final authority in decisions involving the kids.
- If the ex is not around, find out where she is. She may not be involved in the kids' lives now, but eventually she may well be!
- Accept what's in that decree and plan. More than likely, if you want it changed, you'll have to go to court to do it.
- Make certain the ex's name is removed from all your partner's accounts, both personal and professional, as well as all credit cards, bank cards, safe-deposit boxes, life and medical insurance plans. Alternately, make sure that your partner's name is off all the ex's accounts!

Need a Checklist?

☐ Read your partner's divorce decree and custody agreements.

☐ What constitutes the alimony and child support? When will alimony end? (Remember, child support will most likely continue until the kids are eighteen or twenty-one.)

☐ Have you noted your partner's designated time with his kids? What does a weekly schedule look like? Holidays? Weekends?

☐ What is your partner obligated to pay, aside from alimony and child support?

☐ Who has the final say regarding decisions about the kids' schools, sports, activities, health, and general welfare? Mom? Dad? Both parents?

☐ Where is the ex, and what is your partner's relationship like with her?

☐ Has your partner revised all his important financial documents to reflect his separation/divorce with his kids' mother? Has he changed his health insurance, credit card accounts, and designation of beneficiary on life insurance and pension?

☐ Have you asked the questions you want answers to?

CHAPTER 2

Do the Math

LOOK, WE DON'T WANT TO BE CRASS, BUT THERE IS A MATTER of money. Or, you could say, *money matters*. And it does. *Money* magazine discovered in a nationwide survey that 70 percent of "married couples argue about money—ahead of fights about household chores, sex, snoring, and what's for dinner."[*] And that's aside from the financial headaches caused by divorce and custody agreements. When it comes to a monetary discrepancy between your partner and his ex, the amount in question seems almost irrelevant. We've witnessed battles over ten-dollar disputes that were just as charged as ten-thousand-dollar disputes. Money equals emotions, especially in situations regarding divorce and custody.

"Oh. My. God. I don't get it. My soon-to-be-husband and his wife share fifty-fifty custody, but he has to pay her child support as well as alimony? Until the kids

---

[*] Troy Dunham, "Poll: How Husbands and Wives Really Feel about Their Finances," *Money* magazine at Time.com, June 1, 2014, http://time.com/money/2800576/love-money-by-the-numbers/, infographic.

are twenty-one! Come on, it's not like the kids are two (they're eight and ten and in school all day). She has a master's degree, and granted, she has been 'out of the workforce' for ten years, but it seems to me like their 'wonderful, fair-minded mediator' had a bit of a bias here. Am I right? And now I find out that the whole deal is nonnegotiable. WTF?" —Geri

---

So here's the deal: after you've read the divorce and custody agreement, and after you've had sufficient time to take a jog or a high-powered walk and yell to the trees (instead of at your partner), sit down with a family budget planner spreadsheet or even a good old-fashioned pencil, paper, and calculator and record exactly how much money will be subtracted monthly from said partner's income. That amount, depending upon whether you have a joint bank account, will be subtracted from your total presumed income.

"My partner started a college fund for his two kids with his ex back when the kids were little—a legitimate 529 fund that could not be touched for anything except college—and he still maintains it. The ex promised that she, too, would contribute to a college fund for the kids, as she and my partner would split the cost of the kids' college. Well, my stepson is turning sixteen in six months and Mom said she'd give him her old car (as a gift from both parents), and we would pay her half of the Kelley Blue Book value of the car so she could buy herself another one. Reasonable enough. But she finds a car for herself that's a grand more than the value of her old car and tells my partner he has to pay the difference! What? Of course, we said no way to the extra cost, so she countered with, 'Fine, I'll just take it out of his college fund.' Which leads me to wonder what the hell kind of college fund she set up in the first place. In hindsight, the best plan would have been for a legit fund in both parents' names with equal amounts deducted from both parents' paychecks, a real college fund that couldn't be raided when the ex felt slighted." —Camille

Deal with the net income, not the *gross*. (Of course, by gross, we're referring to your partner's income before alimony and child support are subtracted for his ex.) Take a good look at that number, circle it, and then have a little talk with your partner about how much extra money, aside from the court-sanctioned support, will be spent on your partner's ex and their kids. Will he also be paying for weekly ballet lessons and car insurance? Co-pays for doctor visits? His ex's uninsured, biweekly shrink appointments? Her yearly jaunt to England so the kids can visit her parents and entire extended family? What about clothes, birthday presents, school supplies, sports equipment (is a twenty-foot trampoline really a necessary athletic item?), class trips, sneakers (Junior has to have the latest, most trendy Converse alt-vintage-signature kicks on the market)?

"My husband's ex has an extremely generous child-support settlement (even though she's now married to a guy who could fit our entire home in their living room), so one would think that she wouldn't sweat the small stuff—and I mean the really, really small stuff, like a four-buck bill for notebooks—but no. Because the settlement states that she and my husband share the cost of 'extras' fifty-fifty, she comes at him every opportunity with receipts for everything from shoe-freakin' laces to 'seasonal' bike gear. The exchanges were annoying and distracting as they made every pickup and drop-off of the kids about money. We finally figured out a plan. My husband told his ex-wife that he was 'streamlining' his bills, so that in order for her to receive what was due her, she would have to submit *all* bills together, in an envelope, by the tenth of the month in order to be paid. That's it, everything in the envelope, so he could cut one bill a month, which he sent her electronically. No bill in the envelope, no payment until next month. Ta-da!" —Kim

"I learned that sometimes you have to suck it up (if you're at all financially able) when it comes to extra expenses, especially if it's in the best interest of the stepkid. My husband has a pretty comprehensive divorce agreement about splitting expenses, so when it came to his daughter's braces, he split the cost fifty-fifty with his ex. Not surprisingly, the ex fell behind on her portion of the payments—way behind, despite her good, steady income. Even though it was time, after two years, for my stepdaughter's braces to come off, the orthodontist said she wouldn't take them off until the remainder of the invoices had been paid. My stepdaughter waited for her mother to pay so that her braces could come off. After six months of waiting, we finally made the extra payments." —Olivia

Surprise expenses are the things that can lead to resentment, and believe us, you don't want to steer this marriage onto Resentment Road. Discuss your own income and how much you'll be contributing to household expenses. Be proactive on the financial front, not reactive. In fact, now is as good a time as any to start sharpening those nonreactive skills, in financial as well as emotional situations, so as to retain your sanity when those little surprise expenses pop up.

"I knew when my partner and I first started dating that he had a child. I knew he had responsibilities, both emotional and financial. Of course I knew that. And since he has custody of his child and she was going to live with us, I thought that our household expenses would reflect that, in terms of his paying the majority of our expenses. I mean, is it so terrible of me to expect that we split the rent and bills sixty-forty, with him paying the bulk? He thought I was a monster for making such a proposal. God, I wish we'd talked about the money aspect beforehand." —Selena

Best case scenario: everything is spelled out in the divorce and custody agreements, including who pays for the freshly ground organic dog food and glaucoma medicine for the fifteen-year-old, half-blind Pekinese Maxie that lives with the ex. But don't be surprised if there's nothing in writing regarding Maxie's care and maintenance. Often, certain expenses are left unresolved, which more than likely means that your partner (and you) will be paying for them, because your partner doesn't want to rock the proverbial boat. The ex assumes that your partner will pay, so he does, or the ex has made him feel obligated, or worse, guilty. Believe us when we say that half to 99 percent of the crap that your partner puts up with in regard to the ex is out of his own feelings of *guilt*.

Remember? As we mentioned earlier, it may be guilt over the failed marriage, religious guilt over a divorce, guilt toward his kids for not loving their mother, the guilt of friends feeling the need to choose sides, and on and on.

Whatever the case may be, in our collective experience, we've found that the money issues add up not only on the calculator, but also in resentment and anxiety.

"My husband's ex nickel and dimed him about everything when their daughter was younger. Unfortunately, there was nothing in the divorce papers about college—no thinking ahead there. Again, it brought up huge money issues, which were my husband's biggest issues with his ex. Fortunately, he and she were able to decide on a plan to split the cost of college, but my husband always wound up paying more than his fair share. So, about six years later, when my stepdaughter decided to get married, we did not make the same money mistake twice. We opened a checking account for my stepdaughter into which my husband and his ex each deposited the same amount of money so that his daughter could take care of doling out payments for all the expenses, taking us out of the business manager role." —Stephanie

Money is an emotional issue in the best of family circumstances, so just imagine what the stakes may be when there's a pipeline draining out half your family's income. Knowing what's in store ahead of time may not ease the drain, but it will prepare you.

Little (or Not So Little) Legalities

Funny (or not), the legal term for the nonnegotiability of final, court-ordered alimony and child support is "inviolate," meaning safe from violation, untouchable, *permanent*. Don't be scared. There probably is some end in sight, somewhere down the line, but more importantly, it means that it's a total waste of headspace to dwell on those dollar amounts. Accepting that your partner's total expendable income is minus the ex's check(s) is a lot like accepting that spring comes after winter. It's just the way it is. What the ex spends the money on is up to her. As long as she's feeding and clothing the kids, it's her prerogative to post vacation pictures to Instagram of her and the kids on a Disney Fantasy Cruise while you and your new hubby are working weekends and/ or two or three jobs to make ends meet. In some states, however, the noncustodial parent can petition the court to request that the custodial parent (the one on the financial receiving end) provide an accounting of what she's spending the money on. Just be aware of what the support guidelines are.*

And while we're on the subject of the difference in guidelines from state to state, we must stress that agreements in one state may not be valid in another! Please check with an attorney, or take a look at the legal resources for your state, conveniently listed at the end of our book.

"My husband had been paying alimony and child support to his ex-wife for ten years, and I knew that the money often went toward her own lavish hobbies (and procedures). Two years ago, my stepdaughter went off to college, so her mother relocated out of state. My husband's divorce decree states that if either parent chooses to relocate, it must be under very extenuating circumstances; otherwise, they must relocate within one hundred miles of each other. The decree also states that my husband must pay child support until his daughter is twenty-one. My stepdaughter had no interest in relocating or living with her mom during school breaks, so it seemed completely unfair for my husband

---

* Since there are different guidelines for different states, take a peek at support guidelines at http://www.childsupportguidelines.com/articles/art200004.html to see whether your partner is entitled to ask for an accounting of child support monies.

to continue child support, but he continued, because he hates 'stirring the pot.' I made halfhearted protests, but after a year of paying support for a child who was no longer in his ex's care(!), I put my foot down. Of course, it got ugly, because attorneys had to be hired. My stepdaughter was upset because her mother became vicious, but in the end, it was proven that my husband's ex violated the agreement, so he didn't have to pay child support. Case closed. I've advised my stepmom friends that when certain directives are in black and white (and you are aware of them!), you must address those directives and make sure that the right thing is done—the right thing for your family and your finances! This is a time to encourage your partner to follow through. Trust me, we did the math, and it was worth the time and effort to be absolved of three years of unnecessary child support." —Desiree

That little legality of child support—it's based on the annual income of each parent and the amount of time (days out of the year) spent with the children by both parents. Don't even try to discern how to calculate this amount, because the headache isn't worth it. Just know that there is a *formula*, one that's used all the time in the case of child support, and that it varies by state. All you have to do is Google "How is child support calculated in California (or wherever)?"

Child support is traditionally paid by the parent who does not have primary custody, but even if your partner and his ex have fifty-fifty custody, chances are that he will still be paying some child support, most probably until the child(ren) are eighteen (in New York, it's until the youngest is twenty-one, and in some cases, until the age of twenty-two, depending on whether they are full-time in an undergraduate program). This, too, will be spelled out in the divorce decree. The thing is, if the court has ruled that your partner has to pay his ex $2,500 in child support every month, then that's that—*unless* your partner abruptly finds himself without income.

If your partner loses his job, as unfair as it may seem to you, he still has to keep up his child support. That is according to the formula of most child support laws. However, if he truly is at a loss of income and there is no way he can meet his financial obligation (really, *really* can't do it), then he must go back to court with the ex to explain why he can't pay his designated support and try to have the amount *reduced*. The catch-22 here is that it costs money to hire an attorney in order to go back to court. It may be better in the long run for you to pitch in if it's only a temporary job loss. But that's your decision. In any event, it's all the more reason why you need to make sure there is a legal document spelling out the "what ifs" of different financial scenarios. It's also a good argument for keeping separate checking accounts (more on this in a few pages). Remember, if your savings and income are not commingled with your partner's earnings, then your wages cannot be figured into your partner's child support equation, in which case, if your partner has a loss of job or income, he may very well have a good chance in court of reducing his payments.

Child Support for Baby Daddy's Child

Aha! Yes, of course we need to address this, because it certainly is no longer an anomaly for a new spouse or partner to come from a relationship that produced children without a marriage license. Conversely, we don't want to assume that you, in the role of stepmom, are *married* to your partner. Look how long and how many children into the relationship it took for Brad and Angie to make it legal (not, apparently, that it helped in the long run).

It's highly likely that, despite the fact that your partner was not legally married to the mother of his kid(s), there *is* something in writing regarding child support and visitation. In a best-case scenario, the agreement was signed by both parties and confirmed by a judge. If the agreement is not in writing, it will more than likely be discretionary—meaning that it is unbinding and nonobligatory—which can wind up being a financial, logistical, and emotional nightmare. We would highly suggest you insist that your partner revisit such an agreement and make it legal. It will be an upfront expense to do so, but having everything in black and white (and official) will save you money and aggravation in the long run. The lack of a written custody and child support agreement could prove to be a ticking time bomb, one that could devastate your household emotionally and financially a year or two or ten down the line.

Alimony and Spousal Support

Merriam-Webster defines alimony—often called spousal support or maintenance—as "an allowance made to one spouse by the other for support pending or after legal separation or divorce." You may define alimony as the giant thorn in your partner's side and the pain in your…whatever. But as we mentioned earlier, there is most likely an end in sight. There are different types of alimony, depending upon the duration of the marriage, what state you live in, the ages and health of your partner and ex, ensuing hardships, etc. Some support is temporary, and some is more permanent in nature. And how will you know all this? Yup, by reading the decree.

According to the American Bar Association, only 15 percent

of all divorce cases include alimony payments.* If your partner falls into that minority percentage, it is most likely because the ex stood to lose her *standard of living* due to the divorce. It may not seem fair, but it's the law. Accept that the amount is court ordered under the divorce decree and move the heck on. Don't waste another moment dwelling on the amount or imagining "what if." The ex will not only receive the check, but she's entitled to spend it on whatever she deems worthy. Is Botox or Bali in December worthy? Whatever. It's not your concern, because there's nothing you can do about it anyway. The good news for you and your partner is that alimony is tax deductible, whereas child support is not. In fact, the receiving party of child support gets the tax break, since the IRS does not consider child support *taxable income*.

> "There was a time when the ex-wife was so hell-bent on getting additional alimony and child support from my husband that she started court proceedings. Our attitude: Oh, yeah, well, we'll see you in court! When I told the other stepmoms about this, one who had been through the same experience said to me, 'Let's do the math. How much more money does she want each month? How much will you spend on lawyers and court

---

* "Ways to End Alimony Payments," Legal Articles, attorneys.com, accessed October 9, 2017, http://www.attorneys.com/divorce/ways-to-end-alimony-payments.

costs? You know that it will take you a year to get on the court calendar. What about the emotional toll on you and your husband? If she wants $10,000 more per year, and it's going to cost you at least double that in legal fees and weeks or months of your time in preparation, maybe it makes sense to just give her what she wants.' So after weighing the pros and cons of court dates and attorneys, my husband and I realized that negotiating directly with his ex and agreeing to her demand was the best option for us." —Serena

Separate and Equal Accounts?

If you've always had your own checking account, you may be thinking that separate accounts for you and your partner will be your gateway to financial peace. After all, you probably won't want to be continually reminded of all the money he is paying out to his ex. On the other hand, you may want to know what's being deducted monthly in order to keep track of the family's total finances. You may feel the *need* to know, despite what it costs you in anxiety and emotionally induced binge eating.

If either of those options don't seem right, maybe the answer for you is a joint account just for the expenditures that you as a couple have together such as home, groceries, cars, furniture, computers, etc. and separate accounts for everything else—for him, that may mean alimony, child support, and "extras." For you, it may mean vacations, savings, your bio kids' college fund, etc.

"Even without a calendar, I knew when my husband had written the monthly $3,200 check to his ex. He'd walk into the house followed by a trail of black clouds! At first, I thought I'd stave off the storm by writing the check from our joint account for him, but then we decided to have his paycheck deposited in a separate account. Each month, alimony and child support payments are automatically deducted from that account like a mortgage payment. Out of sight, out of mind. No more cranky husband." —Heidi

---

"My husband and I added each other's names to our individual checking accounts when we married. But there's an unwritten rule that we don't write checks out of the other person's account. We have access to each other's statements but view the accounts—and his alimony and child support—as individual responsibilities. Separate checking accounts mean no fighting." —Adrianna

---

On the surface, separate accounts would seem to afford both parties some freedom. However, in factoring in the emotional aspect of money, it may not be a good idea for some couples. *Oh no, you mean there's no one right way to do this?* That's exactly what we mean.

"Separate accounts didn't work for us. Since I was contributing to his expenses, I wanted to know how much money was coming in and going out every month."
—Geraldine

Sometimes, depending on the people involved, separate accounts may foster mistrust in relationships, especially if the purpose of such accounts is not clear. Discuss with your partner the stipulations for separate accounts. What specifically is each account for? Can you see his account? Can he see yours? If you have a joint account, are you going to become totally hung up on every little expense that he doesn't explain to you? Will he do the same?

As we pointed out earlier, if your monies are not comingled, your wages cannot be considered in your partner's child support in the event of a job loss or earning reduction. But then again, there's always an exception to the rule, as the rules differ wildly from state to state. Maddening, right? Check with a local attorney to find out what's what.

Yours, Mine, and Our Estate

Let's talk about estate planning—trusts, wills, powers of attorney, medical directives—and life insurance. We know, definitely not the stuff of a romantic evening with your partner. You may be asking, "Can't I wait on this?"

The answer is, "No, you cannot." Period. If you're already married and have yet to have this discussion, run, don't walk, to your nearest estate planning attorney or do-it-yourself estate planning website. Check out the life insurance options available to you privately or through your job or union. Ideally, this is something that needs to be done *after* you've made sure that your partner has gone through the monumental task of taking his ex's name off of all the bank accounts, credit cards, mortgages, home and car and life insurance policies, utilities, etc. (as we mentioned in chapter one).

Although this may sound like a no-brainer for some newbie stepmoms, you'd be surprised at the number of *veteran stepmoms* who haven't gotten around to making sure these things are taken care of. We've all encountered fellow stepmoms (and bio moms alike) who five, ten, and even fifteen years into their marriages had no wills, trusts, medical directives, or life insurance policies or who had unwittingly assumed their partners made some arrangements.

Estate planning is not optional, no matter what your financial situation is. There are affordable alternatives to professional estate attorneys—which include do-it-yourself websites and government and not-for-profit agencies—that can help set up such planning, just as there are affordable life insurance plans to guard against the unthinkable. Think about it.

"My partner and I worked with a professional estate attorney who explained how to make sure that my money went to our daughter, rather than his ex, should I predecease him. We set up three trusts, because trusts, unlike wills, are difficult to fight in court. Through the years, I learned that whenever there is a legal, financial, or emotional issue that gets out of hand, it's time to bring in the experts—lawyers, accountants, and thera-pists. It was during the attorney meeting that we learned his ex was entitled to part of his social security benefits since they were married for so long. Fortunately, my partner and I had good jobs and could afford the help, but when my sister—who had been out of work for a year—needed the same help, she found not-for-profit organizations that helped on a sliding scale." —Amber

In most states, if you die—again, we know, not the subject you wanted to hear about when picking up this book—without a will, your assets will transfer to your surviving partner. If something happens to him the following day, all your assets may transfer to *his children*. You might want to be clear on what amount will go to you upon his death and what will go to his children. Will there be a trust fund for his children? If so, who will manage it? Is there a third party or trust designated to making the money decisions for all the heirs? If you plan on having children together, what would the disbursement of funds look like then? Be clear, and don't be afraid to talk about money issues, whether you're a newbie stepmom or years into the journey.

"I'd been living with Alex for four years, so I heard all about his contentious divorce. We'd planned to get married...eventually. In the meantime, Alex paid for certain things, such as the mortgage on our home, while I paid for our living expenses. We more or less split our expenses fifty-fifty. When Alex died suddenly at fifty-two, I realized that I'd never seen his will! Why would I ever have thought to look at it or imagined him dying such an early death? Of course, there was no provision for me in his will, which was prepared during his first marriage and never updated. His kids were left every-thing, and I had to move out of our home. It's been awful. What I wish I'd known..." —Gaylen

---

In short, have the discussion about wills and estate planning early on. We understand you may imagine that even *thinking* about the unthinkable is bad luck. Trust us, please—it's not. What constitutes bad luck is *not* having this discussion and not amending certain financial documents.

After you've done the aforementioned and noted what needs to be changed, you might want to focus on your own prenuptial or domestic partnership agreement, the latter of which is a contract that sets forth the understandings between a couple concerning obligations, property, finances, and the like, all of which need to be addressed if you're not married. And like we mentioned before concerning divorce and custody agreements, documents in one state may not be binding in another, so if your partner was married in Ohio, then moved and divorced in Michigan, and the two of you and his ex and kids are now in Florida—whew!—time to check with an attorney or seek legal advice through one of the agencies we've listed in the back of our book.

"Before I married Rick, I knew that he would eventually inherit his family's business, which was small at the time I came into the picture. Rick asked me to sign a prenup that would carve out his family's business from our joint assets, if ever we were to divorce. Well, of course I never imagined divorce, and I was in love.

I didn't want to start negotiating contracts with my future husband, so I signed the thing, as awkward as I felt about doing so. Cut to twenty-two years later after spending two decades helping Rick to build the business into something big and profitable—along with playing stepmom to his kids! Rick left me for another woman and filed for divorce. Surprise, surprise; out came the prenup from twenty years earlier! I'd completely forgotten about it, and it had never been revisited and revised as circumstances changed. Twenty years earlier, I'd quit my job to work for his family business. Eventually, we came to a resolution, but not until we'd spent way too much money on lawyers and court." —Mallory

The Clothes Off and On Their Backs

Clothing can be a big issue between divorced parents, but the one who seems to find this issue most exasperating (no surprise here) is the *stepmom*. It is beyond frustrating—well, most of the issues we bring up here can be filed under *beyond frustrating*—to spend money on nice clothes and have them disappear over a weekend into the void of Mom's house, never to be seen again. This is an ongoing battle for divorced parents of children and teens. Who is paying for all those clothes? If you don't already have kids, you cannot imagine the funds (let alone the time and energy) it takes to outfit a kid who may be growing at a nuclear rate. If you're in a temperate climate (or if winters find you clad like the Abominable Snowman), then we're talking wardrobes for every season and more than likely two sets of each. You wouldn't think that a kid could *lose* a winter jacket and gloves on a freezing afternoon, but they can and do. Who is responsible for outfitting the kids? Does the decree mention this? Most likely, it doesn't.

"My stepdaughter was only three when I married her father, and every weekend we had her at our house, her mother would send her with clothes that were either stained or too small for her. It was like we were the Salvation Army, and the ex was making 'drop-offs' in my stepdaughter's suitcase. I knew that the girl had beautiful, expensive clothes that she wore to school and on special occasions—I'd been to the school and to some of those occasions! There wasn't really much we could do except wait a couple of years until the girl was a little older. Since I'd been a latchkey kid and had to be really independent at an early age, I taught my stepdaughter how to pack her own suitcase when she was five. I told her to pack it with all the things she would want to have with her at our house, including clothes and one special toy. Then I made sure that the clothes were returned to her mom's house. No more 'clothing drop-offs' at our house." —Nancy

I know it sounds as though we are making a big deal over clothing, but it is one of those issues that most stepmoms have argued over with their partners at least once (if not seventy-two times or more). There's no one-size-fits-all (forgive the pun) way to deal with the clothing dilemma, which is why we've included more than a few stories (with solutions) on this topic.

What works in one household may not work in another. Some parents may insist that clothing from one house must stay at that house, and that suits both households. Adversely, if the stepkids must bring clothes back and forth to both households, they may feel that *your* home is only temporary, that it is only a "visit" even if they're spending half their time with you. However, if it's their mother's wish for them to do so, so be it.

"When I became a stepmom of two elementary-aged children, a friend of mine with years of stepmom experience warned me about 'disappearing' clothes, and she straightaway gave me her solution! As soon as I could, I took my stepdaughter and stepson to a luggage store and let them pick out their very own overnight bags. My stepdaughter chose a small, neon-pink suitcase, and my stepson picked a royal-blue duffel bag on wheels, and then I had their names monogrammed on their picks. These were the 'special' suitcases for bringing their clothes back and forth from Mom's house to Dad's, and they loved them. Both children carried those bags with pride and even packed their own clothes. It's amazing how responsible elementary school kids can be when given some incentive." —Julie

Do you have a rule that certain clothes are only for your house? Can they wear the clothes from your house back to their mother's? Or is your mandate set in stone about whether they must leave the clothes you and your partner bought them at your place only? Whatever you decide, just remember that in the end, clothes are just that…only *clothes*. Don't make the kids feel bad for leaving them or bringing them or losing or staining them. In the end, you have to decide, based on your particular circumstances, what it means to, dare we say, *co-clothe*.

"My husband and I are 'clothes people.' It's the one of the few things we splurge on…nice clothes, for ourselves and for his kids. His ex, on the other hand, never uses any of her money (she has a good job) or, apparently, the child support on nice outfits. However, we would never see most of the clothes we bought the kids once they wore them to their mother's house. My husband asked the ex where the clothes were, and she'd invariably say they were dirty or that she'd have them next visit, which never happened. After months of this, we finally got smart and had the kids change back into their clothes from her house when it was time to go home. When the kids got a little older, like ten and twelve, he would say to their mom, in front of them, 'It's okay if the clothes are dirty. Just put them in a bag and bring them to our house on Friday!' Then the kids would get into the habit themselves." —Abigail

---

"Yes, 'child support' means that Mom needs to buy clothes, and yes, it's a drag for the kids to have to pack and unpack every time they go from one parent's house to the next, so the way we solved this with my partner's two children, seven and ten, was with a reasonable compromise. We have the basics at our house, which means clothes that the kids have picked out (we shop at Goodwill, Walmart, and T.J.Maxx), a pair of shoes, a pair of sneakers, pajamas, underwear, and, of course, toiletries too. The kids bring any 'favorites' from their mother's house, and we make certain that they return to her house in the same clothes they arrived at our house in. Sometimes it's an inconvenience, but it's easier for the kids not to have to schlepp their clothes around, and they'll feel more welcome at your house if they have their own set of clothes there." —Sheila

The clothing dilemma happens to be one of those issues that seems more important and more difficult when your stepkids are younger. As they get older, they'll most likely be choosing their own clothes and be more responsible about where they bring/keep their favorite threads. In hindsight, years removed, you may even wonder, "How did I let all that clothing crap get under my skin?" In hindsight, in *years*, you may wonder that, but for now, we understand how frustrating it can be.

TAKEAWAYS

- Know the net income of your household—after alimony, child support, and special and unavoidable extra expenses.
- Accept that *guilt* plays a big part in how your partner acts and reacts in regard to financial matters. Money is *emotional*.

- Don't be surprised by those extra expenses your partner has agreed to pay for (even though there's nothing in the documents about them). Instead, talk about them!

- The child support and alimony is what it is—*by law*. No use questioning or fighting about either.

- In the case of your partner as baby daddy, chances are any agreements, financial or otherwise, are not in writing. Encourage your partner to make those agreements binding and legal in the form of a domestic partnership agreement.

- An accounting suggestion: separate accounts for earnings, as well as a joint one for shared household expenses. Just a suggestion.

- Don't tiptoe around estate planning. Set up those trusts, wills, titles, and bank accounts—with a professional, if possible. And don't forget about life insurance!

- Your stepkids' clothing will probably be a point of contention. Who pays for it all? How does it make the trip back and forth between your house and the ex's? Make a plan, but remember, after all is said and done, it's only clothing.

CHAPTER 3

Rules and (No) Expectations

SINCE THERE IS NO WAY OF KNOWING AHEAD OF TIME WHAT your blended family will be like, it's best to figure out as early as possible what your and your partner's expectations are for your new family. Seriously, this is the conversation to have five seconds after the one about the divorce and custody agreement (well, maybe, like, the next day). And right after you have this conversation with your partner, it's time to share some of those expectations with the kids (if they're old enough) in a family meeting.

This is only the beginning, so take a breath and one step at a time. We'll have more on the logistics, speed bumps, and roller coaster rides of your new family later on in our chapter aptly titled Your Modern Family.

The Family Meeting

It may sound daunting at first—the family meeting (ominous even, if you're a fan of the TV show *Survivor*, as you may be conjuring up images of voting someone off the island)—but think of it as a means to unite everyone. It's powerful and empowering to give people a chance to express their thoughts and feelings. Encourage everyone in the household to participate, even if the youngest is only four or five—if they're old enough to choose their own outfits, they're old enough to have a say. Give everyone a chance to speak and ask questions. Show your appreciation for their participation. The first meeting will be the toughest just because it's the first.

Still feeling a bit tongue-tied on your initial meeting with your blended family? Here are some issues you may want to address:

- How will you and your stepkids introduce each other? How will the child(ren) introduce their stepsibling or half sibling? (Don't get us started on the concept of a half sibling—more on that soon.)
- What will your stepkids call your own mother and father? What role will your family (your mother, father, siblings) play in your stepkids' lives?
- What religion, if any, will be observed in your house? How will that impact the stepkids if their mother is of a different faith (even if she's a howling pagan who is prone to sacrificing small animals on the eve of the full moon)?

- What happens if you and your partner have a baby?
- What are the rules of your new household?
- How are chores to be divided?

Name Calling

By which we mean: What are you to call these new family members? What are they to call *you*? Are you thinking: Do I really need a title? What's in a name? Does my kid introduce my partner's kid as "my stepsib" and our child together as "my real sib, but not with my first dad"? It's complicated, but you get the gist.

It doesn't happen very often, but sometimes a stepkid will immediately fall into the routine of calling you, the stepmom, Mom. It may be stated in the divorce decree that no one other than (bio) Mom and Dad may be referred to as such, but kids have internal decrees of their own. Secretly, you may feel elated, vindicated even, that your stepkid feels comfortable enough and *likes* you enough to call you Mom, but just for a minute, put yourself in the ex-wife's shoes (we don't ask this very often, as those proverbial shoes are like ancient binding slippers). No mother is going to feel good about her kid calling another woman Mom. If your stepkid has a mother who is still in the picture, you may want to remind them that if you're all in attendance at the same event, you're to be called by your first name. Why add gasoline to a small fire?

"When my husband and I first moved in together, my stepson wanted to call me Mom, and he wanted to refer to my older sons as brothers. Well, his mother went nuts about that and would not allow it, so I suggested he call me Elizabeth, although he always referred to my sons as his brothers. My sons from my first marriage affectionately call my husband Stepper. Names are whatever you make them." —Elizabeth

---

Sometimes one small consideration in advance can start you off in the right direction, such as how to refer to the kids when you're out and about, especially if you have bio kids of your own.

Let's say you're out at a restaurant (or a store or a school event), and some well-intentioned person exclaims, "What a lovely family! Are they all yours?" Well, sure, on the outside, that may seem like a simple question, but for you it's a Zen koan! How do you answer without separating the family? You've wanted your kids and your stepkids to refer to each other as "sister" and "brother," as siblings, not half siblings or stepsiblings. Maybe you say, "Thank you, we're a blended family." Or maybe you simply say, "Yes," or "Thank you," and then introduce the kids with something like, "These are Evan and Ben and Robert, and they're brothers." If you trip up and catch yourself introducing your nonbiological kid as your stepkid or your child's half sister, maybe make a note to yourself to simply introduce them by name. Here's letting you know that this will come up—introductions and comments by strangers—and you need not be taken by surprise. Remember, no one's asking you, "If a tree falls in the forest and no one is there, does it make a sound?" You don't need to be stumped by an innocent question.

"My daughter Emma has introduced her stepbrother and sister (from my husband's first marriage) as her brother and sister since she was old enough to talk, but they, six and eight years older than her, introduced her as their half sister, which always made me feel like crying. A few years back, we were in an ice cream store, and the elderly woman manning the cash register asked my stepson, Elliot, the names of his sisters. He said of his bio sister, 'This is my sister, Chloe,' then he affectionately put his hand on Emma's shoulder and said, 'and this is only my half sister, Emma.' Just as I felt my eyes starting to well up, the lady looked quizzically from one kid to the next and said to my stepson, 'Hmm, so which half is your sister, the top or the bottom, or the right or left half?' Elliot looked confused, so the lady continued. 'Well, see, I have an adopted sister, and we never call each other adopted sisters. Just sisters. So you don't need to say half sister, do you? She's your sister, right? So why not just say sister?' Power to Elliot as he nodded his head up and down and said, 'Okay, yeah. That makes sense.' I mouthed to the old lady, 'Thank you.'

Never again did Elliot refer to Emma as his half sister. Although, a while later, I found out from my stepdaughter that one day while referring to Emma as their sister, their mom went ballistic and told them that they either refer to her by her first name or as their half sister. So in their mom's presence, they chose to refer to her as Emma but as their sister everywhere else!"

—Kendall

It's highly likely that just when you think that *everyone* is square on how *everyone* is to be introduced, you'll find yourself at some school function or you'll be picking up your stepkids when another parent addresses you as your stepkid's mother. They assume you're the mother, and maybe not having ever met the mother in person, they call you the ex's name. Make the correction without a fuss and without apology. It goes something like this: A parent says to you, "It's so nice to finally meet you, Erin," or "I'm so glad to finally meet Susie's mom." You say, "Actually, I'm *Carla* Smith. *Erin* is Susie's mother, but it's nice to meet you as well." The other parent is going to feel far more awkward than you. Be polite and laugh it off. Tell them it happens all the time. Make a quick, light correction and move on.

Rules of Your Household

"Different households, different rules. It was as simple as that—well, not so simple at first, especially since the ex allowed unlimited TV and screen time, voluntary hygiene, bottomless candy, rude behavior, and an apparent ban on the words *thank you* and *please*. So my husband and I apologized for the inconsistency in rules between households but not for the rules themselves. My feeling: the rules will set you free. Truly. And they did. As young as his kids were (elementary-aged), they very soon adjusted to the fact that TV, screen time, Snickers, and ice cream were limited and that manners mattered. Clean bodies and teeth were not negotiable, and nothing was gotten with *gimme*. Sure, they would forget some of the most basic rules, but my husband and I would gently remind them, and ultimately they realized that our house was their house and that our rules were important to follow as a family." —Elizabeth

---

There are rules, always, for everything. Don't argue with us—that's *our* rule.

There are even rules in the most chaotic of households. As a parent, you set up rules mainly because you're hoping for a relatively peaceful and smoothly run family democracy—or oligarchy, depending on your own control issues. You want the kids to be happy, well-mannered, thoughtful people, which is what most sane and decent women want for their children, whether they're bio, borrowed, or step. The simplest of these rules for kids include things like: brush your teeth, make your bed, do your homework before having screen time, and if you have a snack, clean up after yourself.

"Everyone needs rules. I learned this after the fact. It's the first thing I advise new stepmoms to address at an early family meeting for their new blended family. One of those rules is that everyone has chores. No one likes them, but there is at least a chore or two that a kid would prefer over another. I wish I'd realized this in the beginning, before I assigned to my stepkids chores that they resented. After a lot of yelling, we all finally sat down, and my partner and I asked his children, who were preteens at the time, and our daughter, who was a few years younger, to choose their own chores. We heard things like, 'I hate loading the dishwasher!' Well, then, we said, 'Since you have to pick two, which chores wouldn't you mind doing?' Them having some choice in the matter worked for us. There were far fewer battles." —Betsy

At the end of the day, there are consequences when rules are broken or ignored. It doesn't matter whether the rule breakers are your kids or his; however, we've found that the most difficult issues arise when the rules for the stepkids are different from the rules for your bio kids. That all said, sometimes, *sometimes*, the rules *are* different for your kids and his.

"Everyone kept telling me that the rules had to be the same for the stepkid and my kids. Well, there are four boys at my house, two from my first marriage and two with my husband. My stepson falls somewhere in between. Talk about not wanting to start an argument—it was a noisy household already! When my stepson was over, he refused to follow the basic rules of the house, such as making his bed and doing his own laundry. I spoke to my husband about this, and he agreed with me, but he just couldn't bring himself to confront his then twelve-year-old son. I wasn't going to take it on either, so when my stepson didn't do his chores and my kids asked why the rules were different for him, I said to them, 'Go ask your father,' and I would pack my stepson's dirty clothes with him to take home to his mother. The only way I could maintain my sanity was to disengage, which for me meant ignoring my stepson's behavior along with my husband's inability to discipline him." —Vanessa

In many ways, kids are more resilient than adults. In time, they'll adjust to the back and forth routine of two homes and even appreciate knowing what's expected of them. (Although, don't expect that appreciation to be noticeable or acknowledged. Remember: no expectations.) Until that happens, it's possible they may think your particular rules suck, especially if those same rules don't exist at their mother's house. Be warned. Know in advance that your stepchildren don't want to be parented by someone who *is not their parent* (i.e., *you*). They probably don't acknowledge their stepparents as authority figures, which means that rules and boundaries should be set up as edicts from *their father* and you. *This is how we do things at our house, even if it's not the same as how you do things with your mother.*

"I can't begin to tell you how many times my stepchildren said, 'At my mom's house, we don't do that.' At first, I didn't believe them. I had to squash my impulse to quip, 'You don't brush your teeth morning and night, take daily showers, and wash your hands before meals?' But the more time they spent in our home and didn't or wouldn't follow basic hygiene, the more I realized that they looked and smelled like they were telling the truth. Initially, my husband and I reached out to his ex with the hope of discussing how we could parent collectively so that expectations for basic hygiene and personal responsibilities (chores!) were the same in both homes. We hoped to explain that it would be easier on the kids if they didn't have to switch gears when going from house to house, but his ex responded with certain excrement-heavy epithets. It became clear that the only time my husband and I could have some positive influence on his kids was when they were with us. There was no way we were going to change the ex's habits or house rules, so it was a tremendously freeing (if not obvious, in hindsight) realization that we could only control what we can control! Thankfully, the kids understand that the rules are different in each home. In addition to taking care of their personal needs, they make their beds every morning and help in other ways without arguments or nasty comments. All of this was possible because my husband and I stayed on the same page from the beginning. If one of the kids said, 'Dad, I don't want to do what she says. Why don't you make your own rules?' my husband responded, 'This is our house, and while you're here, you have to follow the rules that we've agreed on.'" —Kelly

---

"My stepkids had cell phones from a young age, like seven and eight. There was no turning back on that, but the problem was that whenever they were at our house, their phones were glued to their hands, and whenever their mother called or texted, which was about a dozen freakin' times an hour, they responded immediately. It didn't matter whether it was mealtime, homework time, or bedtime. Needless to say, it felt like the whole time they were with us, their mom was making constant interruptions in our family. Even more irksome was that when the kids were at their mom's house, they wouldn't respond to any of my husband's texts. After months of this, my husband asked them, very calmly, why they didn't answer. The kids said that their mom didn't like them responding. My husband and I thought about this for a while. Finally, the next weekend the kids were with us, we introduced the phone bowl rule. From that point forward, when the kids arrived, the phones went in the bowl for homework time, dinnertime, and family time. They could have the phones back for half an hour prior to bed to make up for all their important missed calls and texts. Once my stepkids explained to their mother about the new rule (why they'd missed her 197 texts and emails), she sent my husband a nasty email to which he never responded. As the kids got older, they figured out how to negotiate the disruptive communication (when to ignore a text or call). Takeaway this: you don't have to feed the beast!" —Megan

Step In to the Ex

Once you and your partner have figured out the *proposed* dynamics—remember, nothing is written in stone, and everything is negotiable and will change—it's a good idea to suggest that your partner reach out to his ex and advise her (as a courtesy) of your plans. Although she may not approve (a euphemistic term for "Although she may go into a tailspin and razor-cut your partner out of all the family portraits if she hasn't already done so"), it is in the child(ren)'s best interest that "Mom" is aware of the dynamics in Dad's new family.

It's a respectful move on both your and your partner's part—the outreach to the ex about your household's dynamics—and it sets an example of respect to the children. It also presents you and your partner as a team, which is equally important. This is only the beginning in regard to establishing yourself and your partner as a new team while navigating your personal outreach to the ex.

It's worth mentioning now (and we'll be sure and remind you again later): take the high road in dealing with your partner's ex. If and when possible, be the adult, for the sake of everyone in the room (at the party, on the playground, in the auditorium at the kids' holiday pageant). You don't have to be emotionally invested in someone to be kind and civil. In fact, you should not be emotionally invested in the ex or in anything she does! What you do need to be, for the sake of your own and your family's sanity and emotional welfare, is civil and polite. One of our favorite stepmom role models once said to us, in regard to dealing with a volatile ex: *If I don't have a welt from biting my tongue, then I'm not doing the best job I can do.*

We know, it's the hardest thing for us to not explain and overanalyze, to not try to make right what we think is wrong. We, as women, fix things; we roll up our sleeves, and we want everyone to get along. We apologize. Too much. Which brings us to a topic of particular angst to some of you.

But It Was My Fault

No, it wasn't. If you believe you broke up your partner's marriage/relationship, we'd venture to say that there's a 99 percent chance that the marriage/relationship was already broken before you showed up. If it wasn't entirely broken, there were issues—big issues that weren't being addressed or acknowledged. Chances are that you were the straw that broke the camel's back. A divorce or separation may not have been in full swing, but if your partner's previous marriage/relationship was strong, you would not have been that straw. We can tell you up and down, from now until doomsday, not to feel guilty, that guilt doesn't help any situation—never ever—but you probably won't believe us, and you will continue to blame yourself. Don't do it. There are going to be enough people wanting to place blame on you and try to make you sick with guilt—namely the ex, the kids, family, friends, you name it. Don't toe that line. Yes, the kids especially might be angry, but they are angry for a whole host of reasons that you cannot fix. We know it doesn't seem fair, but it's been shown again and again that kids are more hostile to stepmoms than they are to stepfathers. Resentment, hostility, depression—these may all be by-products of the breakup, and the best you can do is try and be as empathetic as possible. Most importantly, your partner needs to show support of you and affirm his commitment to you as well as to the kids.

"Ugh, I hate reliving this story, but it goes like this. My best friend, Nancy, and I moved back home after meeting our husbands in college. We all became friends, good friends. I mean, our kids were friends, they played sports together, and we went on family vacations together. The whole deal. On the outside, my marriage to Peter looked great—Brady Bunchy— but it wasn't, and in hindsight, I should have initiated therapy, a split, anything other than what I did, which was to have an affair with Nancy's husband, Mike. I won't go into the torrid details, but of course, it ended badly. Nancy must have suspected something, because one afternoon, when she spotted his car outside his golf club—she knew his clubs were at home—she went into the clubhouse bar and found us. I'm sorry to say what happened was right out of a pulp fiction novel. I was in a lip-lock with Mike, and Nancy went postal. She smacked Mike and then pulled me off the bar stool and tried to pull out my hair. Security had to break us apart. It was a nightmare. The divorce took two years, but a year after that, I married Mike. We all still live in the same small community, and Nancy has never forgiven either of us, which is understandable, but she has also never stopped telling everyone within

earshot how horrible we are and what a 'nasty skank'
I am. She has remained the victim, still now, after six
years. And what's so sad is that everyone is tired of her
victimhood and her bitterness, especially her kids. Yes,
it took a lot of effort and soul searching and therapy
to make peace with all the kids, but it paid off. My
ex was devastated, but he eventually came to terms
with what happened and what was really going on in
our marriage. He moved on and married a wonderful
woman, who happens to be an awesome stepmom to
our kids. I am not proud of any of this, but I know that
the end of a marriage is not the fault of one person.
I claim responsibility for my actions, but there were
three other people involved. Sometimes you see only
what you want to see." —Molly

Depending on the kids' ages and the circumstances of your
partner's split with their mother, your partner can decide what information ought to be disclosed to the kids, in addition to the assurance
that the split wasn't *their* fault and that they were not the reason for
the split. He can invite you to join the conversation at some point
in order for the two of you to show a united front and for you to
express your empathy to the kids. Hell, you may even try to reach
out to the ex to apologize for the difficult situation that you all now

find yourselves in. But don't be naive—you may be *rebuffed*, to put it mildly, for your efforts. Your reward is that you are being the adult, the bigger person. Go ahead, do it, but then focus your time and attention on helping your relationship flourish with your partner.

When all is said and done, you are going to feel guilty whether you feel you broke up the marriage or not. Get over it. There's a reason why stepmoms tend to be more depressed than divorced moms—it's because they never stop feeling guilt, they never stop bending over backward to accommodate everyone except themselves, they often don't have a clear understanding of what their role is, and they don't define the boundaries of that role. Be strong, ladies. We got your backs.

The United Front

"From the beginning, my partner and I were a gently unified front. Even if I disciplined my stepdaughter in a manner that my partner may have questioned (I was very new at this stepmom gig), he would *never* correct me in front of her. If anything, he might question my actions later, which would give me time to think about my response for next time." —Stephanie

Remember, no matter where any blame may lie, keep in mind that your partner's kids are probably going to test and retest you, which means that you have to have your partner's support in backing up the rules. He can assure the kids that you are not going to replace their mom, but he also needs to assure them that no matter how they feel, no snarky or abusive behavior from them will be accepted.

Learn how to say no: *No, you cannot talk to me with that kind of language. No, I will not let you disrespect me in my own household.* Or make a deal: *You treat me with respect, and I will do the same for you.* Look, it's a matter of living by the same rules we learned as kids: *Do unto others as you would have them do unto you. What goes around comes around. No act of kindness is ever wasted.* Take your pick, but it has to be the rule at your house, a rule enforced by your team of two, which means that your partner needs to be on board. Between the two of you, mirror the behavior you want back from the kids.

TAKEAWAYS

- Have a family meeting with your new blended family as early on in the game as possible.
- Talk about how your family members will refer to one another.

- Make rules for your household. Know that some of them will be useful, some of them will suck, and some of them will be abandoned altogether, but make them nonetheless.
- Reach out to the ex. There's a first for everything.
- Don't live in guilt and blame. It benefits no one.
- Present a *united front* with your partner!
- No expectations. We mean it. This could actually be a takeaway for *every chapter*, so at the risk of repeating ourselves and for the record: *have no expectations*.

CHAPTER 4

"You're Not My Mother!"

"It sucks being a stepmom. At best, you're always going to be a third- or fourth-class citizen." —Eleanor

---

REPEAT AFTER ME: "I'M NOT MY STEPCHILDREN'S MOTHER. I'm not my stepchildren's mother. I'm not my stepchildren's mother. I'm not, I'm not, but…"

Whammo. And that's exactly where you get into trouble, with that little *but*. *But* I know what it's like to be a mother. *But* I have children. *But* I'm a child of divorce myself. *But* I know exactly the right things to do for my partner's kids. *But* I'm already doing all the chores that a mother is supposed to do. *But* I care. *But* I'm there for the kids more than their own mother is. *But* the kids even call me Mom! No buts matter. Once again, for posterity, you are not your stepkids' mother. Assuming the ex is alive (no snark, please), your stepkids already have a mom and a dad, and if those kids had their own way, they would never choose to be stepchildren in the first place—meaning that they would certainly not choose to have *you* in the picture. (Think about it: your bio kids may have their own stepmom as well, and try to imagine how thrilled they are about that.) More than likely, your stepkids are already resentful that they have to split their time between their mother and father and everyone else in their lives, so they may not be very receptive to giving you a piece of the proverbial pie that is "time with Dad." There may also be an ex in the picture who is more than happy to point out at every possible juncture, "You are not my kids' mother, so don't even try to be!" Well, there you go.

"For the first six months my husband and I were married, his daughter would, literally, kick me under the dinner table when we ate. Know what I did? I changed my chair so that I was far enough away that she couldn't reach me. Seriously." —Stephanie

---

Yes, you're responsible for *helping* your partner raise his kids and look out for their well-being, and yes, you must first and foremost be responsible for a child's safety, but ultimately, decisions concerning his kids are not your responsibility. Oftentimes, your partner isn't even in on the decisions made concerning his own kids, especially when his relationship with the ex is contentious. A lot of times, the bio mom makes the final decision, thereby removing you even further from the process. You may argue: *Why can't my partner and his ex just communicate, at least for the kids' sake?* Well, that's a good one, because if your partner and his ex were good communicators together from the start, they probably wouldn't have gotten divorced in the first place. So let's take that argument right off the table, shall we?

Even if your partner needs your help in making decisions, and even if you are more skilled at parenting than he is, you will still not be the one making the final decisions regarding his children. Even if the ex is perfectly sane and reasonable (ha, fat chance, but *even if*), and even if your partner's divorce from her was amicable, the ex may always be somewhat *unreasonable*, because all the crap that caused her and your partner to divorce in the first place clouds her mind.

> "I do not pretend, *ever*, that I am my stepkids' mother. I am their dad's wife, and at best, I'm their friend. In the beginning, when they were little, it was easier to be 'motherly'—you know, attend the usual events, make lunches, etc.—but now that they're older, the best I can do is be present when they're around, especially since their mother still hates my husband. It's about not getting emotionally attached, truly!" —Jen

Despite the fact that you probably have an active role in getting your stepkids to their schools, medical and dental appointments, Brownie meetings, soccer games, and swim meets, you will also probably have little or no input in any decisions pertaining to those activities and appointments. You will help them do their homework, build science projects, proofread book reports, and remind their father to sign permission slips and show up for school performances (for which there may not be an extra ticket for you to attend).

It can be frustrating and maddening to have such limited input, especially if your views of parenting are 180 degrees different from the ex's. Unfortunately, there's nothing you can do about the ex and her parenting skills. What you can do instead of stewing in your angst is to take a walk and pound out your frustration on your Nikes, or you can grab a coffee or drink with a friend who is also a *stepmom*—other stepmoms understand. Have a manicure, or buy a book to get lost in for half an hour. Walk out the door and drive (or take a bus or a subway). Just don't waste your time running the proverbial hamster wheel in your head.

If you start taking out your frustration on your partner (or the kids), it will color your whole relationship, because there is nothing *he* can do to change the ex and her personal approach to parenting. The ex is who she is, and believe us when we say that *she's* not going to change any time soon just because you think she should.

However, there may be something you can do to help your partner with *his* parenting skills. You may, for lack of a better term, *parent him*. You may have to be the one to set up some of those house rules we talked about, even if they're as simple as the need for respectful behavior and a few nonnegotiable terms of basic household cooperation. You suggest to him that you'll take care of laying out the ground rules so that everyone better understands each other, and all you ask is that he support your efforts.

Then, to the kids: *Yes, duh, you have to bring your dirty dish into the kitchen and load it in the dishwasher, and you can't insult me in my own house. Yup, life's tough, and you can make up your own rules when you have a place of your own (and a servant instead of a stepmom).* Feel free to insert your own script here in your own inimitable words.

If you're certain (for sure certain) given a particular situation that you do, in fact, know better than the ex about what is best, don't jump in yourself to communicate with the ex, especially if you've been rebuffed by her before. Instead, *suggest* to your partner that he take control of the situation himself. If and when he is able to assume control, you may then be free to step in and *help him* remedy the situation. It sounds elementary, but it's sometimes the only way things get done when you're not the mom.

"My stepdaughter had developed warts on her hands and feet, to which her mother responded by saying that they were only pimples. Pimples? You didn't need a medical degree to see that they were warts and that they embarrassed the kid. But I wasn't about to make a suggestion to the ex and be chided with 'It's none of your business. You're not her mother!' so I suggested to my husband that she see a skin doctor. He then emailed the ex, who basically ignored him, so he asked me to make a doctor's appointment during his daughter's scheduled time with us. Sure enough, it was warts, and all that was needed was medication, which, after time, eventually cleared his daughter's skin." —Suzanne

---

Not only mustn't you think of yourself as Mom, but you also may want to try not thinking of yourself as a *parent*. The term itself is loaded to begin with, especially if you have some carved-in-stone textbook idea of what being a parent *means*. Parenting means many different things to many different people—disciplinarian, scheduler, Sherpa, therapist, friend, nursemaid—so as a start, just let go of what you think you're supposed to be. There is no tried and true, one-size-fits-all definition of stepmom. At best, you can be an influential adult in the lives of your stepkids.

"My husband's first wife had an affair and left my husband. They had a daughter who suffered because the mother was clearly taking care of her own emotional needs first and foremost. I met my husband soon after his split, and because the mom was so emotionally absent from her daughter, by my simply paying attention to my stepdaughter, I became the surrogate parent without too much pushback. I showed up. After a couple of years, the mom finally found a little peace of mind and became more emotionally stable. She stepped back into the role of Mom, and I stepped into the role of friend. At first, I was really hurt—disappointed even—but I was reminded of how even the most intimate of relationships change and morph, and it's true with stepchildren as well. My stepdaughter has a great sense of humor, so I was able to go forward in a positive way and appreciate her friendship." —Jasmine

I Hate You

The *best* you can be as a stepmom (and a human being) is positive, caring, and compassionate. That's the ideal. But that may be difficult if the ex has a dartboard with your partner's face as the bull's-eye, or the ex has forced the kids to take sides, or your partner's kids are scheming to get their parents back together. You set up the rules, as we discussed, and you try not to take the sullen eye rolls, the stony silence, and the guilt trips directed at your partner too seriously.

You may succeed in responding calmly when your seven-year-old stepdaughter says to you, "But my mom lets me watch R-rated movies at her house!" or when your twelve-year-old stepson says, "I don't have a bedtime!" But you may not quite be prepared the first time you hear the words *I hate you* directed at you—as in, *I don't have to do anything you say, because you're not my mother, and I hate you.*

"'I hate you! You're not my mother!' Yeah, well, touché. The thing is, the way you react with little kids is much different than with teenagers. When I became a stepmom, my husband's kids were teenagers already. My best friend, who went through the whole stepmom thing, told me that I needed to disengage, big time, that the kids were who they were going to be, and it was too late to try and teach them anything. She also pointed out that I'd hit the proverbial stepmom wall and that the best I could do was to be emotionally disengaged, which meant that I couldn't invest in being the perfect stepmom in order to make them happy. I didn't have to drive them everywhere and do their laundry or clean their rooms in order for them not to hate me. They were old enough to figure it out themselves. Of course, it helped that my husband was on my side." —Desa

---

It's funny how differently words affect us, depending on who's doing the speaking…or the yelling. If your bio kid says, "I hate you," it's brutal of course, but if you're thinking on your feet, you know to chalk it up to hormones or fatigue. When your stepkid says the same or marches out of a room banging doors or stamping their feet, you want to say to someone (your partner, most likely) "What a brat your kid is!"

We're warning you right now, don't say *that*. Think instead that your stepkid's anger is coming from the same place as your bio kid's burst of anger, and it has so much less to do with *you* than their feelings about their current situation. Those moments of "I hate you" are great times to practice total bipartisanship, to harken back to that good old childhood retort regarding stick and stones and *names never harming*. You may even try a response as simple as, "I'm sorry you feel that way, because I do love you." Or "I understand you're angry/disappointed/frustrated, but it's really hurtful to hear you say that." However you decide to combat the moment of "I hate you," just remember to take a breath before you proceed with a healthy dose of *cool*, and keep in mind that your stepkids are just that…kids, and that they didn't ask to be in this step situation in the first place.

The birthing of a stepfamily is super stressful enough without taking every small statement and accusation personally. Take a step back. If you don't do it at this juncture, you are going to be the one to miss out on whatever good comes your way.

"First time I heard one of my stepkids yell at me, 'You're not my mother!' it was like a punch in the gut, but it was the truth. I'm not. And even though I wanted to yell back something equally childish like, 'Yeah, unfortunately for you, because your mother is a raving lunatic!' I managed to say, as evenly as possible, 'Yeah, that's true, but I have your best interest at heart, and when you're here, you have to do as I say.'" —Margaret

As we venture into the stepfamily fray, so many of us maintain a dream of the perfect family, a family in which everyone gets along. Along those lines, you reason: if I love my stepkids and I can get them to love me, then life will be good, and all the stress with my partner's ex will go away, because she will be grateful to me for loving her kids!

That makes sense...but only to you (and in some niche genre of fiction known as family science fiction), because there's a very good chance that if your stepkids do reciprocate the love you develop for them, Mom may feel neglected, threatened, or dismissed, and then you're up against her ire in spades.

We told you that there were no right answers, which means that there is no magic formula to making this instant family of yours a success. There are, however, lessons to be learned from the experiences of those who have trodden this weary path before you, which is why we stepmoms are here for you. You are not alone!

Instant Family?

One day, you're single; the next, you're a family. Voilà! Congratulations! But don't beat yourself up if you're not immediately *feeling the love*, because research shows that it takes from four to seven years for a stepfamily to feel and function like a family (and that's not even clear as to *what kind of family*). To say that there's a bit of an adjustment period would be a gross understatement.

It's like you're squeezing your way down a crowded aisle to your seat in a movie theater and the movie's already begun. You inquire of those whose toes you're stepping on: *Fill me in. What's happening? Who is she? Who is the guy with the gun? What's going on?* But all you get are stares and shushes. Yeah, it's a little like that. The movie's already happening, and you're entering in the pitch dark a quarter of the way through! Or imagine that you're an understudy to a play that's been going on for months and, *bam*, no rehearsals and you're in! You're expected to know the lines, know where to move, be ready for a brutal audience on an opening night that may last for *years*. We're telling you to relax and that you won't know how to do it all, not today and not tomorrow. But we do hope that, with our help, you might sidestep the big emotional land mines and successfully navigate the territory of your new family.

"Honestly, I felt so guilty for the longest time, because as much as I love my stepkids, I don't love them as much as I love my own daughter. It's terrible, right? I mean, I'd lie down on railroad tracks for my stepkids (well, at least one of them), but I just don't feel the same way about them as I do about my bio daughter. Every 'first' my daughter has had in her life, I was there for, but my stepkids came to me pretty much formed, as teenagers, and although we've managed to develop an awesome friendship, it's just not the same. It was another stepmom who gave me permission to accept that truth and make me stop beating myself up." —Louise

---

Let's say that in this instant family, you've covered the important initial issues such as finances, rules, and scheduling. You already know when to expect his kids at your house and which weekends and holidays belong to the two of you. You understand where the ex's responsibility ends and your partner's begins. Next, it's important to be clear with your partner as to what, specifically, *your* responsibilities are with his kids when they're at your home versus *his* responsibilities.

What happens when the kids are at your home and Daddy wants to join his buddies for a game of golf or a beer after work? Are you automatically the designated babysitter? Does he hire a sitter with or without your approval? Are you going to come home to your mother-in-law every time he's late from work because he's asked her to pick up his kids so as not to "trouble" you? When his kids are at your place for quality time with Dad, but Dad is busy, are you expected to pinch-hit? Is he expecting you to do all the shopping, cooking, cleaning, and laundry because that's what his ex did?

Watch out for that last question in particular. Be careful that you don't assume the role of instant nanny, housekeeper, and chauffeur. If that was his ex's primary role, then be careful of stepping in as the understudy! Sure, you're going to pick up some of his slack and try to take responsibility in your role as stepmom, but you don't want to assume anything. The more clarity you gain about your presumed role as stepmom and the sooner you have said clarity, the better.

"My ten-year-old stepdaughter had horrible eating habits, not only in her choice of foods, but the way she sat (lounged) at the table and the way she held her utensils. He said, in so many words, that as a woman, it was my responsibility to teach her table manners. What? Well, I tried to be the etiquette chief. I made suggestions to her for weeks on how to sit/eat at the table, which fell on deaf ears. Finally, I had a word with my husband. We decided that maybe someone else ought to be responsible for teaching her how to sit at the table (because she couldn't hear it from either of us). We sent her to an etiquette program, and she went, willingly! She actually told us how fun it was." —Stephanie

Curb Your Involvement

Look, we, as women—despite our personal ambitions, successful careers, and powerful personalities—are natural caretakers and nurturers. It's part of our strength as women (seriously, if only we ruled the world…but that's another book). We can become emotionally invested in *everything* if we let ourselves, so it's here we stepmoms must jump in to warn [cue screaming siren]: back away from the emotional involvement!

You're going to want to be involved in your stepkids' lives, go to their activities, celebrate their achievements, attend their dance recitals and sports events, help with their homework, take them shopping, be their friend. And we say go ahead. Do it all if you want, but do it with a sense of detachment, meaning that you do it without expecting anything in return. Hear that again: do it all if you feel the need, but do it with the kind of Zen attitude in which you expect nothing in return. Seriously. Because you may get nothing back. No-thing. Nada. Zip. Or you may end up with a genuinely loving relationship, despite some bumpy and disheart-ening beginnings. The point is, expect nothing. Give comfort and support, and by all means, embrace your stepkids' perception of their mother, even if you believe her to personify a cosmic black hole. Keep that perspective to yourself, and give all you can.

Believe us, we wish we'd been privy to this same advice years ago, before stepping into the stepmom fray, before we said, "I do!" It would have saved us all a whole helluva lot of heartache, which is exactly what we're trying to do for you. We understand your concerns. We know you. We *are* you. We know better than anyone that, although you are doing all good motherly deeds, you are not your stepkids' mother. This alone may be the most freeing realization a stepmom can have.

"My stepdaughter joined the Brownies in kindergarten, so I figured that she could use all the support we could lend. I signed up to bring snacks to one of her meetings, which turned into a fun baking and bonding afternoon. Since my husband's ex did not want to neglect any opportunity to trip up my role as stepmom, she called me first thing in the morning after her daughter and I had baked the brownies to tell me that she'd decided to go to the meeting and bring snacks herself. She told me that since she was the 'real mother,' it was her prerogative to go. She then advised me that if I showed up, she would make a scene—classy chick that she is.

Frankly, I would have loved to show up just to make her lose her shit in front of an audience, but I knew that the only one who would be hurt was her daughter, who was already upset that she couldn't bring the brownies we'd made. I stayed away, but I froze the brownies, and my stepdaughter got to partake of her treats for a number of visits. But can you imagine?" —Jacqueline

Your Stepkids' Loyalty Is to Their Mom

Kids often idealize their parents, especially in the presence of a step, and it is *not* your job to rectify this perception. You know how they say not to wake a sleepwalker? Well, think of the kids as talking in their sleep, and be chill about all they say. Their mother may be the most reprehensible and manipulative person on the planet, but you will not win if you side against her. Instead, be the person to whom the kids don't have to defend their mother. Lay back. Be the listener. Accept your stepkids' perception of their mother, because you will win nothing by saying anything against her, no matter the circumstances. Understand that the stepkids may even be trying to build a wedge between you and your partner in deference to their mother. They may be doing it consciously or unconsciously, but recognize what it is, and don't take the bait, even if one of them says to you, "My mom is a supermodel who can leap tall buildings in a single bound, and my dad will probably die without her." Recognize the bait, for it can be subtle or outrageous.

> "I feel lucky that my stepchildren are great kids. They're young teenagers, and they're sweet and respectful, but I still feel anxious every weekend in preparation for their visit. Why? Because their mother is so freakin' controlling. She bad-mouths their father, but he never says a bad word about her, which, I must say, is now really paying off. His oldest child is nearly sixteen, and he's realizing how crazy and sabotaging his mother has been. He's said to his dad, 'You know, Mom is always talking badly about you, but I think it's really cool that you and Avery never say anything bad about her.' Smart kid. Great dad. And I can even give myself a pat on the back." —Avery

Most importantly, understand that no matter how horrible the ex is, she is still your stepkid's mother. Think of the complicated relationship you may have had or still have with your own mother. Can she push buttons on you that are unknown to anyone else in the civilized world? Has she ever been annoying? Sure, but God forbid someone else says something negative about her! If *you'd* defend *her*, then you'd better believe that your stepkids are going to do the same in regard to their own mother. It's hard, we know. If there weren't kids involved, your partner's ex, most likely, would never be brought up in your current relationship, and she certainly wouldn't be the stronghold that she is.

It's a strange, crazy-making thing to be constantly reminded of "the perfect, better ex," i.e., "Mom." Your stepkid may be *saying*, "My mom makes the best brownies," or "My mom knows more than you." But what you may imagine *hearing* is that your partner's ex is better than you. Don't go there. Remember, it's just a kid defending their mother.

"More often than not, the kids pay for the resentment between divorced parents or for any acrimony between the ex and the step. On several occasions, I heard my usually kind stepdaughter let fly the most cutting words to me. One night, in particular, when she was younger and I was lying beside her in bed, she said to me, 'My mommy hates you.' My first impulse was to wallow in a pool of self-pity, thinking that everything I'd done to be the perfect parent/friend to this little girl was being undone. But then when I looked at her face, I wanted to cry for her. I realized that she was the victim, not me. I put my arms around her and hugged her and said that grown-ups sometimes say things that are unkind, out of anger. I told her that it was okay if her mom felt like she hated me, but that I wouldn't love her (my stepdaughter) any less. My stepdaughter is sixteen now, and she hasn't forgotten that night, and neither have I." —Amber

Alone Time

Just like you need time alone with your partner (more on that later), your stepkids need one-on-one time with their bio parents. That *emotional detachment* we mentioned earlier? Summon it up wholeheartedly, and encourage your partner to spend some time alone with his kids when they're with you. A lot of stepparents feel threatened by their partner's relationships with their children. Within such a relationship is a history—maybe even a whole different sense of humor or a different language even—a stepparent can't compete with. Remember, his kids have been with him their whole lives! Yeah, think of that. Of course they may have favorite, shared jokes and may like to reminisce on special times and shared moments together. Don't give in to your own insecurity. Encouraging your partner and his kids to have some hang time together will show the kids that you are not in competition with them, and it will show your partner that you understand his needs as well. Revel in the alone time, ladies! Refuel. Revive.

"When my husband and I got married, I had two sons, and he had one from his previous marriage. Together, we had another boy, so there was a lot of jockeying of schedules. My husband was fair in his affections among the boys, but when it came to discipline, you would have thought his son from his first marriage was made of glass. He wasn't afraid to discipline my boys or our son, but he couldn't seem to wield any authority over my stepson (aptly nicknamed 'Little General' by a close family friend), who resorted to tantrums when he didn't get his way. Fortunately, as clueless as I sometimes felt as a stepmom, I knew enough to make sure that each child had time alone with each parent, which meant that my boys had time alone with me, and Little General had time alone with his dad. And then I employed a little professional help to get my husband on the same page as me when it came to disciplining all the boys! Working through our family dynamic wasn't an easy road, and though LG (now eighteen) still has some behavioral issues, what seemed to help was making sure that he had that time alone with his dad." —Ella

"My husband and I collectively have four girls, three of whom are teenagers from my husband's previous marriage. The fourth is our five-year-old, who is positively delighted by a household of girls. We're lucky in that we all get along and that the age difference in my stepkids and my bio daughter alleviates any competition, but the teens do want time alone with their dad. My solution to keeping his girls (and myself) happy was to encourage him to take just his girls on a vacation. He did. He came back happy and a bit worn at the seams, but more important, he was very appreciative of all I did for his girls. And I secretly delighted in staying home with my daughter and doing whatever we wanted to do. No loads of laundry and big dinners; no cleaning up after everyone. My daughter and I ate Ding Dongs for breakfast, Cheez-Its for dinner, watched cartoons and movies, and had a blast. When the rest of the family came home, we realized how much we missed each other (mostly). It was a great renewal of energy and appreciation." —Betsy

Not a Parent, But Maybe a Friend...Sort Of

There's a fine line in this one, remembering that you are the adult, a person in charge, first and foremost the partner of your stepchild's father, not a friend-friend, but a friend. Got that?

There are aspects of friendship that are part of being a parent or stepparent, but as a stepmom, you are in a unique position to bond with a stepkid in a way that a mother or father can't. If you can maintain your boundaries and avoid becoming (too) emotionally invested—yup, sorry, harkening back to ye olde dose of *emotional detachment*—you'll be on your way to finding the formula for a potentially lovely relationship.

"I worked on the friendship side of my relationship with my stepson, because his mother was so nasty to me and didn't want me 'interfering.' She was vicious, and I knew my stepson was a little afraid of upsetting her, so I'd ask him how he was feeling, what he was up to, and I didn't break confidence. The couple of times I relayed a story to my husband were when I thought my stepson's well-being was at stake, and even then, I made my husband act as though he'd gleaned the info on his own. My stepson loves his mother even though he's afraid of her, so there was nothing I could do except be present. When my stepson was in middle school, my husband and I had him tested for ADD (I'd had a feeling about it), and sure enough, the doctors thought he would really benefit from medication. My husband's ex refused to let him take any medication, so the best I could do was let him know what was going on so that he could make his own decision in a few years. He said to me, 'Well, at least I know! And I'm glad there'll be something I can take if I want to when I'm older.'" —Lanna

Establishing a friendship can also give you the opportunity to have a positive impact on your stepkids' lives, which, trust us, never sucks. It may also take the pressure off trying to be a parent. Imagine yourself maintaining a friendship with the children while their parents are busy being parents. It doesn't mean that you don't establish rules or take adult responsibility for the kids' care and safety, and it doesn't mean that you expect any less respect or appropriate behavior. What it can mean is a way of dealing with your stepkids that makes life less difficult for both of you.

"I have to say that I think stepmothering is one part parenting and two parts friendship. I'm lucky in that I have a special relationship with my stepchildren. They keep me apprised of what's going on in their lives, and they share things with me that they feel too embarrassed to share with their parents. Although my partner sometimes admits to feeling left out, he's very glad that his kids and I have this kind of relationship. If I share with him something that the kids have told me about, he understands that what I tell him stays between him and me. If there is an issue that needs addressing, we figure out a way to handle without the kids feeling like I've broken their trust—usually, that means urging them to share with their dad. As far as the 'parenting' part, when his kids are at our house, I do their laundry and pack their lunches for school. I tuck them in bed at night and sit with them if they're not feeling well. It's what I would want if I had kids spending time with a stepparent." —Jacqueline

As a stepmom, you're in a unique position to be helpful in ways that a parent can't. Maybe that means you are privy to things that a parent wouldn't be. Maybe it means you can offer a suggestion or means of guidance or a point of view that is helpful or even refreshing. Say your stepdaughter wants to learn how to cook, and your best friend happens to be a cooking instructor, or maybe your stepson wants to play an instrument, and neither of his parents have a musical bone in them, but you're an accomplished amateur musician, or maybe you're the perfect tutor in computer science, because you've always been a computer nerd, and your partner and his ex don't know the difference between a code and a cipher (neither do we—so don't ask). Look at you, stepping in and offering help! But if you do want to offer time, lessons, or anything that may cost money and involve permission from your partner or his ex, be sure to run it past your partner. He, in turn, can run it past the ex if it will involve her.

"At thirty-eight, I found myself in a second marriage to a man with three teenage girls. I arrived intact with a five-year-old and a demanding full-time job. Maybe because I hadn't an ounce of spare energy, I was able to make the practical decision to be 'friend' to my husband's daughters. I mean, at fifteen, seventeen, and nineteen, they are pretty much adults, and in making the decision not to try and parent them, I'm able to enjoy them in a way that their parents can't really. I don't judge them (but I will admit to praying for them) when they tell me in confidence of their escapades. Although I've always been pretty open in talking about sex with them, I'd forgotten just how crazy teen girl talk could be! They don't tell me anything that would lead me to worry about their welfare, but if they did, I would have to talk to their father about it—fortunately, they have a great relationship with him. When the girls are all PMS-ing together, I know enough to let them bitch and cry, and I don't take any of it to heart, although sometimes it means an extra glass of Chardonnay at dinner." —Amber

---

"I had good advice from a stepmom friend of mine

not to try so hard to be a friend or parent to my new stepson. In the beginning, I listened a lot. I listened to what he talked about with his father and what he seemed interested in. And I asked questions. I learned that my stepson loved movies and theater and music, so I started out by buying tickets to a touring musical that happened to be in town. I would ask if he'd like to see a particular movie. If my husband couldn't make it, we went together anyway. It became the interest that we shared, and no surprise, our relationship developed from our shared interest." —Natasha

The thing is, as a stepmom, you can't afford to overstep your boundaries, because if you do, you will set yourself back months. It's not like simply going back to square one; it can actually put you behind where you were at the beginning. You have to at least start out as a friend to your stepkids, especially if you're looking to have a loving, long-term relationship with them. Don't let the role of disciplinarian fall onto you. That's your partner's job (remind him, *gently*, of this fact). It's hard enough to try to form a relationship from scratch and to earn the trust and respect of a relative stranger without having to take on the role of warden.

"I hate the title of stepmom. It just conjures up all these

stupid old stereotypes. It's such a trap. My therapist told me right in the beginning of my relationship with my husband that women tend to blame themselves when a stepfamily goes wrong. She said that I had to make sure that my husband took care of his kids' needs when they are with us, especially since I'm a 'problem solver' to a psychotic degree. But I think that all women are! So right now, I'm just 'Jessica' to the kids, their father's wife. We'll see." —Jessica

---

Build the relationships with your stepkids slowly, as you would take the time to build a relationship with anyone of consequence in your life.

"My stepdaughter never yelled at me. Instead, she would go silent. If she'd been a friend, I might have cut her some slack and imagined that her way of dealing with anger was to not deal with it. Instead, because she was my stepkid, at first I took her behavior personally, and I felt hurt. It was only after our relationship developed I learned that was her way of expressing anger at something I said. I learned to creatively rephrase the question or statement, and it worked! She still gives me the silent treatment after all these years, but I know now that is just the way she deals emotionally. When she doesn't get back to a text I've sent, sometimes I realize that it's simply a matter of rephrasing my question or 'advice.'" —Stephanie

Partner, All Aboard!

Key to your successful role as stepmom is having an emotionally supportive spouse/partner, fiancé, boy/girlfriend, etc.! Your partner needs to back you up, cheer you on, listen to you (especially when the stepkids aren't), and do the right thing by you and your blended household. Now, since no one likes to be told what to do (or say or listen to), this request (need) for support may be something that you want to bring up organically or in a discussion during a relaxing dinner date with your partner. You must emphasize the need for his or her support, whenever and however you bring up this issue. Sometimes you may even need to be somewhat stealthy in the way you consult your partner.

"My partner likes to initiate things. He wants to be consulted, not admonished. Like, I wouldn't say, 'We're going to such and such's house on Saturday.' Rather, I'd ask, 'Do you want to go on Saturday?' Same with issues concerning his daughter, especially money matters, the

greatest source of stress for us as a couple. I would say
to him, 'Do you think it would be a good idea to let her
[his ex] know that [fill in the blank]' or 'Maybe it would
be easier if you emailed. Then you don't have to hear
her voice.' Suggestions, not solutions, worked in our
case." —Stephanie

Equally important is for your partner to let his kids know
that, first and foremost, not only does he love *them*, but he also
loves *you*, their stepmom, and that you're there to stay. Secondly,
the kids need to know that they must treat you with respect, the
kind of respect that's due any parent—hell, that's due any well-
intentioned adult. Period.

Your partner may push back and say, "Of course my kids
know I love them. Of course they know I love you. Of course they
must respect you. Of course, of course." *Humor me*, is what you
then tell him. He mustn't assume that they intuitively know all that,
and even if they do, these are ideas that need to be reinforced—not
once or twice but consistently.

Stepmothering is harder than mothering *and* stepfather-
ing. Studies have found that while adult stepkids may be happy
about Mom remarrying, they are much less happy about Dad
doing the same. In fact, Dr. Wednesday Martin wrote in an article
for *Psychology Today*, "Stepmoms are frequently singled out for

very bad treatment indeed by stepchildren who pick up on their mother's anger and resentment and become her proxy in their father's household."* Aha! No kidding. Just another enlightening example of the stacked deck against us stepmoms.

"The most effective way to communicate with my partner is through 'coaching.' I learned the hard way that confronting or blaming him or barraging him with questions like 'Why is she such a bitch?' were completely unproductive. Duh. I realized that he was getting grief from both ends, his ex and me! So now when I have an issue, I choose my words carefully. I ask him 'What options do we have?' and 'Did you give her an alternative time to pick up the kids?' etc. Communication became positive, despite the subject." —Kendall

---

In effectively communicating with your partner, you can let him know how best to support you and demand respect on your behalf. At the very least, the two of you can be on the same page about what you have control over (like, your household) and what you have absolutely no control over (the ex). It's also important to realize that your partner is probably doing the best he can with the tools that he

* Wednesday Martin, "Stepmonster," *Psychology Today*, accessed October 9, 2017, https://www.psychologytoday.com/blog/stepmonster/201106/why-its-easier-love-stepfather-stepmom.

has. Oftentimes, there's very little he can do when the ex is manipulating his kids' emotions or schedules.

Frankly, the most annoying questions we hear from our nonstepmom friends are, "Why do you let *her* [the ex] do [such and such a shitty thing]? Why do you let her get away with that crap [whichever crap it happens to be]?" The answer is that you, the stepmom, can't control your partner's ex any better than your partner can! Chances are he'd be happier if he never had to deal with his ex again, so choose the times wisely when you say to your partner, "It's time for you to step in now. It's *your* child. *You* have to resolve this issue." At the same time, it is important that you don't continually assume the burden of the ex's bad behavior, because if you do, your partner will expect you to do the same again and again. He'll assume that you'll take the lead, and he won't do his part.

"I dealt with my stepson's temper tantrums day by day. He was spoiled rotten and had no discipline at his mother's house. When he was at our house and he refused to do what I asked or was combative, I thought it was my job, on my own, to figure out a way to deal with his anger. After a while, I realized that it wasn't my job, and I could choose not to engage. I said to my husband, 'You have to take over now.' And he did! Interestingly enough, although my stepson was extremely disrespectful to his

mother, he was very rarely rude or vulgar to me, probably because I wasn't as invested as his mother. I think it
helps that I don't like being angry. My choice is always to
move on, especially if it's an issue that I can't change…like
my stepson's behavior." —Elizabeth

Stepping Away from the Stepkids

You can't fix something you didn't break, and sometimes the break is within the kids. Sometimes no matter how hard you try and how many solutions you come up with, there is no remedying an unfortunate situation. Hostility and resentment toward a stepparent can manifest in a lot of ways, one of which is a continued power play that, despite your best efforts, seems never to get resolved. When the stepkids are young, you commit to making the family work together, but sometimes, as they get older, you realize that you have to let go.

"It's been years since I married my husband, and being a stepmom to his kids went from a combination of tears and trauma to a respectable working relationship among us all. Early in our marriage, I read something about how it takes four to seven years for a stepfamily to function as a normal family. I assumed that was the case for every other family, not mine. It took a long while for me to learn that my family was not the exception to the rule. Well, the kids are teenagers now, and my stepdaughter and I are close. My relationship with her brother, my stepson, while not warm and fuzzy, is at least respectful. I can be happy with that." —Keisha

Every stepmom we talk to admits there comes a day when she realizes that she's out of steam—a day when she feels like nothing and no one can help her in her role as stepmom.

It's the kind of day that leaves you wondering what the hell you've done wrong the last several (or dozen) years. After all, you've done all your goodly stepmom duties. You've even tried talking to the ex and asking her to reconsider her attitude on, well, pick a subject— holidays, family get-togethers, school pickups, etc.—all for the sake of the children. Even your partner has made a decent attempt at working out a solution with his former partner, to no avail. It is, you feel, the moment right before the revolt, but we're here to tell you that revolt is not the way to go. You've hit the proverbial wall (more on this later), and the change you must make is within yourself.

Our last (well, maybe not the last) word on dealing with your stepkids: move in slowly, carefully, and with an open heart as well as an open mind (and maybe an open bottle of your favorite

Cabernet), and be patient with yourself and your family. You'll find your groove through trial and error, and, we hope, with help from our own experiences.

Even though we stepmoms formed our own like-minded collective and often vented about the same general topics (kids and exes), we all tried different approaches to stepmothering when we were starting out. Since we had different permutations of "family" and different expectations of what exactly "family" meant to us, it took a little longer for some of us to find the happy mediums in our families. You will find yours as well. We're rooting for you.

TAKEAWAYS

- Repeat after us: "I am not my stepkids' mother." Again, louder: "I am not my stepkids' mother."
- Focus on what you can control. Better yet, *know* what you can control and what is waaaay out of your hands.
- There are *your* rules vs. Mom's rules. Don't confuse the two.
- Discuss with your partner your involvement in his kids' lives. Decide together what your involvement will look like, keeping in mind that your stepkids are ultimately your partner's responsibility.

- Take time for yourself by having your partner spend some quality time with his kids—*without you*. Preserve your sanity. It's okay to step away from the stepkids.

- Remain calm with your stepkids. Bite your tongue. Detach emotionally. In other words, take lots of deep breaths. Ommmmm.

- Be a *friend* with a parental touch to your stepkids, instead of a disciplinarian. Let your partner take on that role. It's their job, not yours.

- Communication with your partner is key. He needs to have your back!

- Slowly, but surely, you will find a happy medium. But remember, have no expectations about what that will be.

CHAPTER 5

Your Modern Family

MODERN FAMILY. THAT'S YOU, YOU AND YOUR FAMILY! Just like that hysterically funny yet painfully honest and revelatory Emmy Award–winning TV mockumentary comedy series! Right? Except that in the series, they have a little thing call the "punch up." Oh, yeah, that's when they bring in the joke writers to make sure that every one of those painfully honest and revelatory moments results in a laugh. Just like in real life, right? If only we real modern families were so lucky. *Hello, modern family, this is Mason, and he's going to be inserting some jokes into that horrendous stepfamily moment that happened at cousin Sheila's bat mitzvah.* Modern family.

If you're not crazy about that term, there's always *blended*— extended, mixed, stirred, "frappéed." Blended, sure, especially if you love a good metaphorical cocktail of say, fruit, Legos, doll limbs, crushed glass, smelly Converse sneakers, expletives, and salt (just a few of the ingredients of your new family). The thing is, this new modern family of yours, however you may like to refer to it, is one very complicated animal. While you take the time to welcome your new children (your stepkids), you must also realize that those children come complete with their own accessories in the form of a mother (and possibly her spouse or boy/girlfriend), grandparents, aunts, uncles, and cousins. And don't forget, there are also the coaches, teachers, friends, and acquaintances that form the periphery of your stepkids' lives. What we hope to illuminate in this chapter are the ways in which this wonderful new family of yours might function, the obstacles you might come up against in a typical (or atypical) day in the life of said family, and what solutions there may be.

With your new family come holidays, graduations, weddings, and other milestones (celebratory and otherwise) to which your stepkids may be invited *without you*. Or maybe you'll be invited, but your presence will be ignored. Or maybe the whole family will be included by default but separated by blood relatives and stepfamily. In any event, to paraphrase the wise and wonderful Dr. Seuss, "Oh, there will be places to go and things to see," with, perhaps, a few added complications in getting to those places and seeing those things.

Chances are that you've heard—or some well-intentioned friend or family member has *warned* you—to beware: second marriages have a higher divorce rate than first marriages, and if the kids have problems (anger, depression, substance abuse), those problems are going to be tenfold in the stepfamily. Contrary to that wisdom is a study showing that "the divorce rate among remarried families is high in the first two years, then it slows down. By about the five-year period, second relationships are more stable than first relationships."* Not only that, those second marriages show great benefits to the children. Since we stepmoms have been in our second marriages at least twice as long as our first marriages, we'd like to shoot those early naysayers a few noisy, wet raspberries (among a bunch of single-finger gestures) and offer some key topics and solutions for *your* modern family.

Logistical Nightmares and Solutions

Don't be the last to know. Anything. Even though it's your partner who ought to be privy to his kids' schedules and events, 99 percent of the time, it will fall to you, as stepmom, to know what's going on in their lives. We've found that dads are less likely to take action—sometimes it's just their way of trying to keep the peace, or they want to remain "the good guy" or the Disneyland Dad.

If the ex is pulling outrageous stunts, your partner may even be likely to give in to her, which is why you have to step in. If the ex is being stingy with the details of the kids' schedules and activities,

---

* Virginia Rutter, "Lessons from Stepfamilies," *Psychology Today*, May 1, 1994, https://www.psychologytoday.com/articles/199405/lessons-stepfamilies.

and especially if she's downright hostile about sharing information that *needs* to be shared with *both* households, then it is important to be creative about garnering said information. This is especially important when the kids are young and everything is planned out for them.

"On days my partner has custody of his daughter, she attends the school's after-school care program because he and I both work. Routinely, in lieu of being with her, I would call her at the program and discuss her homework and ask about her day. After a few months of this, the ex found out and told my partner that she didn't want me calling her daughter! I thought it stupid and petty (I would call a lot of things she did stupid and petty over the years), but my partner thought it better not to fight this particular battle, so he gave in. The next time we had custody, I picked up my stepdaughter from her after-school program, and she told me how upset she was that I hadn't called. I felt horrible, but I explained that I did not call because her mother did not want me to, and her father and I wanted to respect her wishes. My stepdaughter said that it was important to her that I call and that she wanted me to keep on doing it. This was where I stepped in and argued the point with my partner.

He realized it was in his daughter's best interest to listen to her and not her mother, at least on days when we were on the schedule to take care of her." —Claire

---

"Time after time, I tried to bring my stepson into the mix of our family, but his mother pushed back by always being hours late. No email, no text, no call, and no response from our calls. Finally, we moved on. We'd write in a text or email what the family plan was (mind you, these plans were on *our* weekend) and what the departure time would be, and we'd stick to it. If she didn't show up on time, we left. The games were done. My stepson was eight, so we explained to him that although we wanted to include him in our plans, we needed to leave on time, and if he wasn't there, we would leave anyway. We were careful not to blame his mom, but she got better when she realized the disappointment it was causing her son." —Frannie

---

Make sure that the stepkids' schools and clubs have both your partner and you listed as emergency contacts and as designated drivers in the case of pickups and field trips. Don't assume that the ex will list your partner and you on applications and information sheets and keep you updated on parent meetings for Brownies, Boy Scouts, soccer, school fund-raisers, or any other activity the kids are involved in. Let their teachers *and* class mothers or room parents know that you and your partner both want to be involved. Check that you're on the tutors' contact list, the doctor's, the orthodontist's. Check, recheck, double-check.

"When my stepchildren were in elementary school, notes and announcements went home in backpacks. Sometimes they made it to our house, but most often they didn't, resulting in a mad scramble when we'd find out last minute about a school function: a play, party, bake sale, 'crazy hair' day, etc. Repeated phone calls to the school office provided only temporary resolution. One weekend, after a total clusterf*** of missed school events, angry calls, and late-night tears, I vented to a family member who happens to be an elementary school principal. He said, 'Go to Staples. Buy the biggest box of envelopes available, put stamps on them all, and self-address them to you and your husband. Then have him (as you have no legal guardianship per the custody decree) bring the box to school and divide it among the teachers of his kids, requesting that all correspondence be duplicated and mailed.' Voilà! Honestly, the teachers were happy to comply, as it was in the best interest of the children; besides, it was no secret to anyone at the

school that my husband and his ex did not communicate well. It was a relief to all involved!" —Julia

If, for whatever reason, your partner is reluctant to step up to the information plate, you may ask him if he'd like for you to step in as his email surrogate. If he agrees, then you have license to compose a letter on his behalf and on his email account to whoever needs reminding that he, too, is a part of his kids' lives. Remember, though, not to make it a habit of picking up the slack. If you have to step in, don't fool yourself in thinking that the teacher, coach, or ex, in particular, doesn't know that you are the one emailing. Women tend to have a much different style than men, in emails as well as texts. Now's not the time to practice being the fiction writer you've always wanted to be.

"Let's be real. Most women are responding for their husbands. The women are the ones composing the emails and signing their partner's names. I think every-one knows this, because it's ultimately the women who are the organizers, the ones who are keeping track of the day-to-day activities of every member of the family. Go on; ask your husband where his seven-year-old needs to be at 3:45 on a Thursday afternoon. Chances are he won't know but his wife will—wife meaning you, the stepmom! I handled *all* my husband's back and forth with his wife. It was so obvious that early on, his ex actually responded with 'tell Caroline that was a really good email.' As conniving as his ex can be, at least she has a germ of a sense of humor." —Caroline

"I had two teenagers from a previous marriage when I married Bill. He had two kids, and then we had one together. I was fortunate to have learned with my own kids that they needed to be responsible for their own stuff. The last thing I was going to do with five kids in a household (two part time) was micromanage. The rule was: everyone was responsible for what was important to them—this from about age eight and up. We told all the kids, if you want your father and me at your game/ practice/performance, then you must mention it to us. It gave them a sense of independence, and it took the pressure off keeping up with every little scheduling issue. Seriously, do the kids need us to go to every damn practice they have? No, I don't think so. The biggest event was and is high school graduation. That's on my calendar." —Cheenu

Lean Away

We already know that you're going to overcompensate for being the stepmom. Seriously, it doesn't matter who you are or what you think your natural inclinations are toward children—you are going to want to do too much and be involved in more activities than you actually have time for. You'll think you have to go to every basketball game, birthday party, and middle-school talent show to demonstrate your involvement and the unified front of your new (and intimidating) household. Easy does it, at least until you figure out whether the situation really warrants your involvement or whether it might be less stressful for all involved if you sit this one out. It may be the perfect time for you to take the time for yourself, to step away and refuel.

"The best thing I can do as a stepmom is be as supportive as possible of my partner's relationship with his seven- and ten-year-old daughters. That also means that it is his responsibility to discipline them. It alleviates anxiety between their mom and me and cuts down on tension between the girls and me. In the beginning. I tried so hard to 'fit in.' I bought them gifts and baked their favorite desserts, but they really turned their noses up at me. So I figured I had nothing to lose by leaning away, so to speak. I stepped back. I was warm and encouraging but way more dispassionate and detached. Eventually, they did start coming to me...to play a game, or watch a movie, or just to talk. I think what they gained was some sense of control of their situation, and it made them more accepting of their whole situation and me. It's definitely a work in progress." —Lex

Don't go to the camp's visiting day if you're going to be competing with bio Mom and Dad and stepsiblings. Let your partner do that one. In fact, let him take your kids as well. Make it a "Dad with *all* the kids event." Sit it out. The same goes for the birthday party at the ex's house. Let your partner go with your kids and the stepkids. It will probably be the break you need, but we'll talk more about that later.

"I learned to detach from the decisions my husband makes about his children that have nothing to do with me. When their needs don't compromise our lifestyle or our relationship, I step back. I don't need to worry myself over those particular decisions. Being in a stepfamily doesn't mean that you need to be privy to every single thing that he's buying or doing for his kids. It's okay for each of us to do things for our own children without each other's permission. I learned to choose my battles, basically. I mean, is it really worth getting pissed off because he bought a sofa and chair for his daughter without my 'permission'? If he can afford to buy things for his daughter and it doesn't affect our lifestyle, then why shouldn't he? Boy, that realization made my life so much easier." —Heather

---

Remember, you are not the cause of your stepkids' angst, so don't take their disruptive behavior personally. Hell, if you can manage, don't take *anything* personally. It's not *you*. Embrace the stepkids, but go on with your life. Make plans, do things, have fun. Show them how to do the same.

A Time for Everyone

Interestingly enough, sometimes in the making of plans and the *doing* and the attempts to find fun time for everyone together, you realize that a little compartmentalization goes a long way. No matter how little time there may be in the day and how many children are in the mix (yours, his, yours together), it may serve you well to formulate an equation in which everyone gets his or her own special attention.

We don't mean that your partner needs to take his kids to Six Flags in order to have some quality time. Time formulated can mean a special bedtime ritual (books, chats, storytelling) for one kid and a trip to the art supply store with another. It's about the time together, not the destination.

"My husband has had fifty-fifty custody of his daughter, Sophie, who is now fourteen, since she was sixteen months old. Two years ago, when my husband and I had a child together, the household became more hectic and then even more so a year later when I had my second child! My husband started to feel guilty about his time with Sophie being divided again and again. What happened is what I call the Sophie effect. When Sophie would come to our house, all normal activities shifted. Time seemed more precious to everyone, especially to my husband, so he would give all his attention to Sophie because they missed each other so much. I kept stepping in and trying to find something for the 'whole family.' I didn't know how to step back. I felt jealous, and I felt ridiculous that I felt jealous! After a while, I realized I had to communicate this to my husband (in the calmest, most nonaccusatory manner). I told him how ridiculous I felt but how much I wanted for everyone to be happy together. We talked a lot about it. We were able to carve out occasions for 'their time' and for 'family time,' and even hired a sitter for 'our time.' Errands and chores were relegated for the non-Sophie days. Our kids got the bedtime stories, and he and his daughter watched *Twilight Zone* reruns afterward. We figured it out. A year or so ago, when Sophie was in seventh grade, she had a homework assignment to write about someone who affected her in a positive way but didn't know they had. She wrote about me and about how she valued my opinions. It still makes me cry to think of it." —Jennifer

In between family time and your partner's "special" one-on-one time with his kids from his former marriage, *your* child(ren) may feel unintentionally slighted. Sometimes everyone's attention is so focused on making everything right by the stepkids that your child(ren) with your partner wind up with sloppy seconds in the "quality time" division. This is one dilemma that, with any luck, you may be able to nip in the bud as soon as you recognize it.

"My daughter was starting grade school when I realized that her father (my husband) was treating her differently than he treated his kids from his previous marriage. My husband had a very demanding job and traveled a lot, so when he was home and his kids were with us (which was half the time), he would be the classic Disneyland dad, carving out special time with them and making plans to do fun things. When it was 'only' our daughter, he'd get home from work and retire right away to his home office to catch up on work. For a variety of reasons, I wanted us to go to family therapy, and one of the therapist's recommendations was for my husband to plan quality private time with our daughter, something as simple as a playdate in the park, time making pottery, or a bowling date—a special weekly time for them alone. At first, he basically dismissed the idea (I think he felt a bit guilty and defensive), but after a few heated conversations (and a few tears on my part), he agreed, and immediately I could see the benefit to our daughter." —Maria

The sooner you set aside quality time, the fewer hurt feelings all around. And while we're on some very important *F* words...

Feelings

Even under the best of circumstances—which means having a communicative partner who not only has a healthy relationship with his kids, but with his ex as well (an anomaly, at best) and who understands his day-to-day responsibilities with his kids—you may not only feel overburdened and overwhelmed in your new *modern* life, but you may also be wondering where exactly you fit in.

You may think that you just don't feel the same way about your stepkids as you do your own child(ren)—*gasp!* As we mentioned earlier, it's perfectly natural not to feel the same way about your stepkids as you do your bio kids. It happens, and it's a very tricky subject. A lot of people, including the so-called experts, will disagree with us. You may find yourself shamed if you share these feelings with others, but it's an important truth to acknowledge. You may indeed love your stepchild(ren) and want the absolute best for them, but the feelings you have for them may not be on par with how you feel about your own kids. That, in itself, is a tremendous and important realization, because the "pitch" is that as mothers, as *women*, we are expected to love all our children, bio and otherwise, equally. It's like some female creed passed down through the ages that no one has ever questioned. Not to do so is downright alarming, psychotic even.

Accept that you do (or will) feel differently about your stepkids than you do your bio kids, and the sooner you acknowledge that, the less inebriated you may need to get. Along with that, accept that your partner *does*, indeed, love his own kids unconditionally.

Give yourself time to get to know your stepkids. Do not, as

we said earlier, think of yourself as "Mom." You're not. Period. If you need to think of yourself in some role, then think of that role as "coach." As the best coach you can be, you will not criticize your partner or his kids, because criticism only serves to set up his and their defenses. If you're blending two families, not only will you need time to get to know your stepkids, but *your* kids will also need time to get to know their new siblings. Rules need to be the same for both sets of children living under the same roof (even if they're only together part time). It will never help to complain to your partner, "my kids would never do what your son did!" or "look how much messier your daughter is than mine!" Being observant and not on the offensive will lead to your own constructive insights, which you can then introduce in equally constructive and sympathetic ways. Remember, be constructive, not critical—actually, a good piece of advice no matter who you are. You and your partner are a team, albeit a new team figuring out new rules and boundaries, but a team nonetheless.

"My husband came to our marriage with his young son, Aidan, and I had a daughter, Regina, from my previous marriage. What I learned is that you can never criticize your stepchild in the same way as your biological child. If Regina was dressed in a too-short skirt, I could easily say, 'You're not going to leave the house like that, are you?' But I would never say to Aidan, 'You need a haircut and a shower!' even though he often did." —Emily

---

Even when a child is, literally, in your family, he or she may not *feel* as though they're family. Sometimes it's all your partner can do to manage his kids with his ex, let alone the child(ren) you have together. It may be that your partner is often absent for dinners because of a demanding job, but he somehow finds a way to be with the family at least when his stepkids are visiting. To him, those family dinners with what he calls "the whole family" are the most important. Unfortunately, that can send a message to your bio kid(s) that they/she/he (and you) aren't "enough" of family to make an effort to be home for that one important time of day, the evening meal, a time when families have a chance to interact and bond. Your bio children need to feel that they're family whether or not the stepkids are there. Key your partner in on this.

If you're having a hard time making your partner hear what you have to say about your kids, therapy or counseling may be very helpful—hell, therapy and counseling can be helpful when dealing with any difficult elements of your modern family. We're big proponents of going outside the family for help. If a therapist isn't in the budget, then perhaps a minister or friend or coach can provide unbiased feedback. The truth is that counseling can benefit all involved, but only when "all" are on the same page.

"My husband, Jim, had two kids from his first marriage, and together he and I had a daughter, Gabriella. For the first few years of our marriage, Jim had a very all-encompassing job schedule, so he'd often miss our family dinners. That is to say that he'd tend to miss the dinners that were 'only' Gabriella and myself. He'd always manage to make it home in time for dinner with the 'whole family,' which sent the message to our daughter that she wasn't enough by herself. My therapist helped me to talk to my husband about this in a nonaccusatory manner. It helped!" —Jenny

"My husband's work sometimes makes it difficult for him to make plans. However, whenever my stepchildren were at our house, he always made it home for dinner and special occasions, and instead of working late into the night, he'd find the time to watch a movie or play a video game with his kids. I insisted that my husband go to therapy with me because I felt like our son (a few years younger than my stepchildren) was being treated like the unwanted stepchild. My husband was shocked to hear that. He just didn't see it, but he came with me despite his reluctance, and the therapist was able to help him see his behavior for what it was. She had to give him exercises to help make his youngest child (with me) feel like he was enough (without the stepkids), that we three alone constituted family. My husband really hates for anyone to tell him what to do, but to his credit, he listened and followed the therapist's advice. Small victory." —Esther

His Ex and Your In-Laws

Do your partner's parents and family still see the ex? That's fine (maybe), as long as they accept you as part of the family as well. Sadly, in some cases, your new in-laws make their preference for the ex obvious, and the ex eats it up *(grrrr)*. It's upsetting, hurtful, and disappointing for both you and your partner. If, for whatever reason, the ex gets invited while you go ignored, it is up to your partner to try and remedy the situation. It may be time for your partner to wean his parents from the ex.

As difficult and downright maddening as your in-law's dismissive behavior may be to you, and as much as you'd like to call them on it, you must remember that these people are your partner's *parents*. Be respectful of them. Go ahead and attempt a direct communication of your own, but by all means, keep it respectful.

"I finally had enough! My mother-in-law was horrible to me for years. After hearing about yet another lie she'd told my husband about me, my ability to ignore her came to an abrupt end. I called her, and I said, 'Do you not realize the wedge you're driving between you and your son with your ridiculous accusations about me? I don't enjoy our relationship, so I would be more than happy if we didn't have one at all. Just for the record, I've been extremely tolerant of your bad behavior, but now I'm done. I wish you the best.' I was shaking afterward, but that night, she called and apologized, and we were able to have a civil relationship from then on. Sometimes the risk of being brutally honest is worth it—that, of course, after a long while of conscious detachment!" —Amber

If you're not making headway in the warm and cozy department with your in-laws, it is imperative that your partner speak up and let them know that you are here to stay and that you are to be included in any family holidays or other special days as a part of the family. Your partner needs to make sure that you are not left behind.

"When my stepkids' grandmother passed away, our twelve-year-old biological daughter asked if we were going to the funeral. I wanted to say, 'Hell, no!' but instead, I said, 'I don't know. Why?' She said that she wanted to go in order to be there to support her brother and sister. Since the grandmother had been nothing but rude and nasty to our daughter and me, her funeral was the last place I wanted to be, but my daughter didn't see it that way. It was a lesson to me: sometimes you have to swallow your pride for your child. We went to the funeral—although I couldn't get the image of a farmhouse atop legs in striped stockings and ruby red slippers out of my head." —Brittney

---

As far as your family is concerned—meaning your mother and father, aunts and uncles—it's the best of situations if they can embrace your stepchild(ren) and include them in family get-togethers, especially the big holidays. If you're reading this book, your new partner has arrived in a package deal, children included, so no matter how dismissive your partner's former in-laws may be of you, your family has an obligation to welcome those children as they do your new love. Look, situations change. Your stepkids may wind up sharing holidays with you and your family maybe only once a year. Let your family know that it's important to you to make it work.

"My stepdaughter was always with her mom for Thanksgiving and Christmas. It was just the two of them. Thanksgiving and Christmas for my husband and I meant big extended family celebrations, and I felt bad that my stepdaughter missed them. But I realized that the mom was probably guilting her into the two of them being together. When my stepdaughter was in high school, she was finally able to make her own choice about where she wanted to be for the holidays. She chose to be with us." —Katrina

Gifts for Mom?

Is it up to you to help your partner's kids pick out presents for their mom? If the kids are little, someone has to help (or at least encourage some small kindness). Is your partner expecting you to figure out Christmas, birthday, and (gasp) Mother's Day gifts and cards? Usually, that's a job for Dad, but sometimes he'd rather take a needle through his cerebral cortex. Go ahead, Stepmom, take it on. The kids will see that you are being generous, friendly, and helpful (whatever!), and you can pat yourself on the back for taking the high road *without* having to actually interact with the ex. This is a tough one, we know, because you may not be rewarded with anything in return—not a gift on *your* birthday, or a thank you, or even a card from those same kids on Mother's Day.

Of course, *someone* ought to remind those stepkids of yours that a text or wish of "Happy Mother's Day" to you (a card even?) would be much appreciated. After all, they probably wish everyone else who they know to be a mother "Happy Mother's Day!"—their neighbor, aunt, grandmother, the waitress serving omelets at brunch. However, it may never occur to them to wish the same to you. Be prepared.

"Newsflash: Do *not* expect a Mother's Day card from your stepchildren. Just don't. And don't guilt them about it either, because that will only net you a future kick in the teeth for 'hurting their feelings.' Yup, your feelings don't matter, because you're the grown-up. That's the train of thought, but trust me, year after year of receiving no thanks on Mother's Day for all the things you do as a 'substitute mother' is like hearing nails on chalkboard. My advice to you: let it go (this is a big one to accept). It's an obnoxious, made-up holiday that was invented to sell greeting cards, and even if you have the best relation-ship in the world with your stepkids, their loyalty to Mom is the driving force in buying that card or gift. It has no bearing on who you are to them. Accept. Move on. It's one day in a year. Go to brunch. Take a walk. Step away from the dirty pile of laundry. Call a fellow stepmom and wish her a Happy Mother's Day. Move on." —Nancy

If you find yourself with an uncontrollable urge to wrestle the ex whenever she's within striking distance and you just can't bring yourself to help the kids shop for her birthday gift, then gently remind your partner, with enough time to spare, that he has some shopping to do. Send him out with the stepkids for some quality shopping time together while you treat yourself to a mani-pedi.

"When my stepson was old enough to ask to 'get something for Mom' for birthdays and holidays (but too young to 'get something' on his own), I would have a little art session with him—feathers, glitter, paper, glue—and let him go crazy making whatever type of card or 'invention' he wanted. When he got older, he started making cards for me as well. His own reasoning: 'You do a lot of things like a mom, so you should get cards, too.' Note: lay out extra newspaper to catch all the glitter that will be glued by the gallon and then will proceed to fall off all over the house. Just saying." —Beth

---

Reentry from Mom's House

And while we're on the subject of quality time and mothers, one of the gripes we all had in the beginning and often hear about when talking to stepmoms is that the hardest time to be with the stepkids is right after their time with Mom. We've all wanted to scream, "Houston, we have a problem. It's *reentry*, and we're burning up!" Burning. Up. Like, no matter whether the mother was the strictest type A control freak or a Disneyland mom who held weekend-long parties with no enforced bedtimes or rules, when the kids came back to our house, they would usually be at their worst, which meant their *meanest*. Sometimes it was because Mom spent the weekend brainwashing them against their fathers or us, and sometimes it was due to the fact that the kids were so damn tired from their unstructured visits or from the anxiety of schlepping back and forth that they'd simply fall into cranky default mode.

The trick is to be aware of this phenomenon and to come up with a plan to combat it, whether it's a special routine involving family games or quiet time (depending on the ages of the kids) or pizza night out. And remember, it's often not just the stepkids who are making the bumpy transition back into your household. There's a chance that your bio kids are also feeling anxious knowing that their routine will be disrupted and the vibe in the house is about to shift. Kids are intuitive; they will sense *your* anxiety in addition to experiencing their own. Maybe you're not even aware that you have, in fact, been growing anxious in anticipation of the stepkids' Sunday reentry. Maybe you've been picking fights with your partner (more so than usual), and your kids have noticed you banging the dishes a little more loudly. Take stock.

> "When his kids came back to our house after a weekend with their mother, I'd literally have to 'de-Mom' them. Not only did she make it known to them, again, how young and dumb she thought I was, but she would let them basically stay up until midnight. We're talking about kids in fourth and fifth grade! I'd been told that cops take showers after their shifts to decompress and wash off all 'the crazy,' so I figured I'd try that with the kids. (You've heard of a Silkwood shower, right? From the movie of the same name, where the lead character tries to decontaminate from plutonium?) Sunday evenings, as soon as they'd return to our house, I'd tell them to go take a shower, or I'd run them a bath. I'm telling you, they were changed kids after that. I don't know if it was the water, or the standing/sitting meditation aspect, or the negative ions…and I don't care. But it worked! They would return to their lovely if overly energetic selves." —Caroline

Stepkids Are Stepkids,
Even When They're Adults

You would think that adults might have learned a thing or two that they didn't know as kids—for proof otherwise, we could provide you with long, harrowing stories about our husbands' exes—so it shouldn't come as a shock to you that adult stepkids may be just as likely as prepubescent teens to give you grief about your role as stepmom. It's not just young children who may have a hard time reconciling themselves to a parent's divorce and remarriage. Adult children can be equally mournful and even hostile, and it probably has nothing to do with who you, the new stepmom, are. You would think that an adult child of divorced parents would be happy to see one or both of their parents happily involved in another loving relationship or marriage, even. You would *think*, right? But oftentimes, loyalty to Mom, feelings of competition, or personal, unresolved emotional issues far, far beyond conscious control come into play in an adult child's dismissal of a stepmom. Listen up: you didn't break it—meaning your partner's former relationship—so it's not up to you to fix the damage caused by it.

"Recently, I turned to a friend for sympathy, because my partner's twenty-five-year-old daughter was acting especially asinine. My friend, who is thirty-five and still angry at her dad for divorcing her mother (years ago), said to me, 'You're barking up the wrong tree, because my dad just got remarried, and now I hate him. I don't give a shit about my new stepmom and her kids. I have no desire to be one big happy family.' What an eye-opener. No, it didn't make me like my stepdaughter more, but it gave me a bit more perspective and an ounce more compassion for her. The girl is mean-spirited and a total user, but I realized that there's nothing under the sun I can do about her behavior. It has nothing to do with me personally!" —Sally

---

"I tried, believe me. I tried for years to be loving and accepting as possible up to the point when my husband's thirty-year-old daughter told him that she never wanted to see me again (this after I asked her to please call her father and ask how he was feeling after surgery, instead of calling to ask for more money—although I didn't say that last part). When my husband told me this, I simply said, 'Okay, that's fine.' Sometimes it's best to go silent, so I stopped intervening. I stopped trying to run interference to the point that he finally saw just how nasty she was. He had spent an evening alone with her and came home and said to me, 'God, she's selfish. It's so annoying to be on the receiving end of her bullshit.' I nodded. He'd finally gotten it." —Sherry

---

Some of you have been doing your best for years to make a family out of his kids and yours, and some of you are in the beginning stages of trying to make it all work. For the most part, your chances of success are good, but there's always the chance that if you're making headway with one of his kids, you may not be making headway with another. Sometimes, just sometimes, there's a child who is hell-bent on making you and your partner's life as miserable as possible. No one likes to say this aloud, but sometimes there's a stepchild who enters your life so damaged and accusatory that no amount of understanding will help. And if his or her parents haven't been able to quell the evil, you probably won't be able to either.

"I met my husband twelve years after his divorce, when his sons were teenagers. Yeah, they were mean and resentful of me from the get-go, but I walked into my new family with an open heart and acceptance of who they were and how they felt. Today, I have a wonderful relationship with the two oldest and their partners and children, but I have no relationship with the youngest, who, at thirty-two, is extremely resentful of his father's happiness. Because he is so unhappy (for reasons having nothing to do with me or my husband or our family), my husband feels really guilty and tries to 'fix' him, which means that he still pays for his car, gas, cell phone, and sometimes his rent. It's not easy to accept this or to intervene, but because I appreciate my life with my husband, I accept that he has his own karma to work out with his son. I don't have to be part of it. I only have to remain supportive and loving of him. Talk about 'letting go'; it's an ongoing process." —Emily

Let's say you're planning a little event for which you're making invitations. And let's say that your stepkids are all grown up and have flown both nests. We'd like to remind you that you don't owe it to them or anyone else to be hostess, mother, and caretaker. Whatever you do, whenever you reach out with an invitation, do it out of the sheer Zen of giving. Expect nothing in return. Nothing. Hell, maybe instead of a reciprocal invite, you'll score an unanticipated enjoyable experience elsewhere.

"In an attempt to make my newly married stepdaughter's life a little easier, I invited her and her husband and his parents to Thanksgiving dinner at our house. That way, she'd only have to negotiate dinner with her dad (and me) and one with her mother and stepfather. She appreciated the gesture—and not having to eat her mother-in-law's cooking. We did that for a few years until one year, my stepdaughter asked if they could bring a couple of cousins. I said, 'Sure.' Well, one cousin was utterly obnoxious and monopolized the conversation for the entire night. The next year, we weren't sure what to do, as we didn't want the cousins back for a repeat performance, so we decided only to invite my stepdaughter and her husband. Instead of coming to our house, my stepdaughter hosted Thanksgiving dinner and invited her mother and stepdad instead of us. I wasn't about to sweat that one. Instead, my husband and I went to Florida for a little R & R!" —Natalie

Not My Circus, Not My Monkeys

You may have heard this proverb before. If not, we present it to you as the perfect mantra in understanding that when all your best efforts fail, you must realize that a problem is not yours to solve, that it's someone else's job to deal with it. In terms of stepmomhood, it's realizing when not to intervene or interfere with

decisions involving the stepkids or the ex. Hands up in surren-
der and say, "Not my circus, not my monkeys." We can't quite
remember which of us first heard it or what battle-scarred elderly
stateswoman of a stepmom told it to us, but it grabbed our imagi-
nations, to be sure. Feel free to make it one of your mantras, when,
after trying to instill certain good judgment or a sense of fairness or
kindness in your stepkids, after attempting over and over to teach
them right from wrong and show them how to act in the world,
they act as if they hardly know you (or your children).

"My husband's son from his previous marriage, Joe, has
behavioral issues. When he'd come home from school,
I'd give him a snack and then expect him to sit down
and tackle his homework before the TV went on. Joe
lied that he didn't have any homework, that he had
done it in school, or that it was none of my business.
My husband always gave him a free ride and even went
so far as to do Joe's homework for him when he came
home from work. He never disciplined Joe. When our
son was in elementary school, however, my husband
was always riding him about homework, grades, and
other things. One day, the lightbulb went on. I realized
if Joe's parents didn't care about his homework, then
neither did I. At the end of the day, all a stepmom can

do is suggest parenting advice to your husband. If he doesn't take it, don't beat yourself up. Make every effort to remain uninvolved and neutral." —Trisha

Those Special Times

We're talking about those celebratory times, though they may not be so celebratory for you. These are the times that come up again and again to the point of nausea, thus the Latin: *ad nauseam*, which, loosely translated, means to continue to bend over backward while banging your head against the wall in your efforts to be loving, reasonable, proactive, and helpful to such a point that you are nauseous. We're not saying that all celebrations won't be fun. We're simply warning that some may be more *trying* than others. We're talking birthdays, communions, bat mitzvahs, holidays, etc.

"My husband and I were at my stepdaughter's house to celebrate her one-year-old's birthday along with the 'biologicals'—which is how I refer to the ex-wife, my two other stepchildren, and the assorted cousins and aunts. Another of my stepdaughters was chronicling the event by taking photos with the really nice, expensive camera that her father and I bought her for Christmas.

As usual in these awkward extended-family situations, my husband and my bio daughter and I were sitting on the sofa talking among ourselves. The photo-taking stepdaughter was walking around getting everyone to smile for the camera...everyone except us. She actually took pictures of the people on either side of us as she went around the room. My daughter said to her, 'Can I get a picture with my sisters?' Now I can't begin to tell you how that chokes me up, my sweet daughter wanting a picture with her generally dismissive older stepsisters. The photo-taking step looked at her and said, 'Maybe later.' My daughter wilted, I teared up, and my husband waved his hand and said that it wasn't a big deal. That's how he copes. But there were no pictures of the 'sisters' or us. Same thing happened at my husband's grandson's christenings. Pictures of everyone, except my husband (and me). He acted like it didn't bother him, but he's gotten good at that demeanor. I, on the other hand, continue to be flabbergasted. I want to say, 'Not anymore...' but only time will tell." —Susan

---

Imagine that you've invested inordinate amounts of time and psychic energy in your stepkids' activities only to be given no mention and no expression of appreciation at their bat mitzvah, communion, or graduation ceremony. Imagine then that *everyone*, it seems, including the school janitor, is mentioned in a particular speech when it comes time for them to "thank all the people who helped me get to where I am." It can be demoralizing, we know. So, going forward, if you don't want any more surprises, have Dad step in and ask his darlings just whom they will be acknowledging and/or inviting, unless, of course, you've hit that final wall (more on this in chapter nine) and you no longer care if you or your child(ren) are mentioned. In fact, if you've finally reached that nirvana of detachment, you may not even care if your stepkid acknowledges Spider-Man in lieu of you.

"When my stepdaughter was in middle school, she was cast in a local musical at a professional theater. It was a big deal, and it meant lots of rehearsals and additional classes and coaching before and after school, weekdays, and weekends. I was more than happy to drive her back and forth, bring her rehearsal meals and snacks, and help her study her lines. Come opening night, my partner, our daughter, and I go to the show, where, of course, we see the ex-wife's entire family. In the lobby are eight-by-ten glossies of the cast members on a wall along with their bios and thank yous to family members. On her bio, my stepdaughter gave special thanks to her mother, her grandmother, her aunt, uncle, cousins, and everyone else on the planet except for me, her father, and her sister. I felt like I'd been punched in the gut. Of course, I wasn't going to spoil my stepdaughter's big event, but after it was all said and done, I asked her why we weren't included in her thanks. She told me she had included us, but her mother made her delete it. I explained how hurtful the omission was and that if the same situation came up again, she should let me know in advance. Her mother's terrible behavior gnawed at me for weeks, but I had to let it go and use the experience to teach my stepdaughter to communicate better."

—Beatrice

"At my stepdaughter's graduation, my husband and our young son were, of course, invited, but only because there were 'extra' tickets after my husband's ex gave nearly all the allotted tickets out to her family and close friends. My husband has a good relationship with his daughter (as do I), but she never likes to take her dad's side when she's with her mother. Apparently, her mother also helped her with her graduation speech, because when she got up to mention all the people who had helped her get to this important moment in her life, she mentioned her mother, her aunt and uncle, a cousin, her grandparents, and a guy named Manny, who, for all my husband knew, could have been her mother's darn auto mechanic. My point is that she acknowledged everyone except her father and me and her brother (my son). I like to think that I was ready for the slight, but it still hurt. The really crappy thing was the omission of her brother. Thankfully, he was too young to notice, but still. The ex also made plans for a graduation party that didn't include us.

We learned enough to know that when my stepson was getting ready for his graduation, my husband—with my gentle encouragement—made sure his son knew how important it was for us all to be included. We were able to plan our own celebration with him. I learned that you don't take any situation for granted. If the ex has behaved selfishly throughout your marriage, she's not suddenly going to be on her best behavior for any occasion, no matter how important it is." —Kerry

If you've tried and tried to fit in at the family parties and still find yourself gulping that extra glass of Chardonnay in a quiet corner, you've got to ask why you would put yourself in another uncomfortable position if people aren't genuinely happy to see you. Why are you doing the awkward maneuvering and excusing bad behavior when your partner isn't? Life will go on if you're not there. Trust us. You're already involved. You've done the dirty work and have run the daily grind, so what if you skip that "big deal" event. Nothing's big enough for you to be intentionally hurt or dismissed, especially if it's not a big enough deal for your partner to take the lead.

"My stepdaughter, Sloane, has been in my life since she was eight. I've schlepped across town with her for every practice, rehearsal, playdate, and doctor appointment she needed to be at since I married her father. I wanted to be involved and an active stepmom in her life—I made her lunches for school, provided advice, stayed up with her nights she was ill, included her in every family vacation and celebration along with my own child, Sophie, who is five years younger than Sloane. My husband's ex tried every which way possible to mess up plans I made, but I plowed through. A few months before my stepdaughter's sixteenth birthday, my husband and I started asking her how she wanted to celebrate. She kept skirting the issue, saying that she didn't know. Closer to the date, she said that she thought she might do something really low-key, like dinner with a couple of close friends, and her mother would take them out. Fine...until the day after her 'dinner.'

She was at our house, and I asked her how her little party

went. Well, excited as she was, she started showing my

daughter (her little sister) and me all these pictures on

her phone. Everyone was at the so-called little dinner,

all her friends and cousins, the grandparents, her aunts

and uncles, even my daughter's babysitter! I thought:

Are you f-ing kidding me? Still, I remained calm, and

later, I told my husband that I'd had it. The party was

the biggest dis possible, not only to my husband, but

also to my daughter and me. I was livid. A few weeks

later, I said to Sloane, 'Mandy, Sophie's babysitter, went

to your dinner (which really was a party that she chose

not to tell us about), and your cousins, aunts, uncles,

and twenty close friends.' But no invite for your sister

Sophie? Huh! Her answer was that her mother felt

Sophie was too young to go, along with some other

nonsense about needing additional adults to be drivers

to get all her friends from one location to another. Clearly

no mention of the fact that she lied to me and her dad!

I At that moment I realized then that my stepdaughter's

bio mom would always win and would always be in battle

against everything I did and tried to do for the benefit

of my stepkids. Sadly, she was too afraid to stand up

to her mother even when she knew her mother was wrong. From that moment after, my priority was my daughter, and to hell with trying to make holidays, trips, and celebrations inclusive and try to work with the ex. The hurt that my daughter felt was beyond gut wrenching. Because of that incident, I learned that my partner didn't have the balls to take on his ex. It took quite a long time to recover—personally and with our relationship—but will honestly never be forgotten!"
—Marina

We know you want to be "bigger" than that/them/the mom/ the stepkids by putting on your best face and braving a potentially unpleasant situation, but sometimes self-preservation is far more important. Send your partner. Send the kids. Send your regrets, if you want. Here's the permission you may need. Then take yourself to a movie—a dark comedy about a stepmom who behaves badly and everyone loves her for it. Go ahead. Find *that* one.

"My partner's grandson was turning five, so my stepdaughter was having a big party for him with all his friends and their parents, and my bio daughter had offered to help watch the kids in the bouncy house they were renting. I bought gifts and wrapped them in the birthday boy's favorite superhero wrapping paper! A couple of weeks before the party, my partner went to his daughter's house, and when he came home, he seemed a bit distracted. When I asked him what was wrong, he said that his daughter had told him, 'There's not going to be enough room at the bouncy house for extra people, so if you could come alone, I would really appreciate it.' *What?* Seriously, I thought I would throw up. I can't even tell you how hurt my daughter and I were. When the next birthday came up, we received what I knew to be a 'mercy' invite, so my daughter and I very politely declined. I even called my stepdaughter to say that her father would be coming alone because I didn't want to cause anyone discomfort (she argued that we were always welcome). I knew that either way, the stepkids were going to talk about me behind my back. Sure enough, when my partner showed up, his daughters (my stepdaughters) read him the riot act about how inconsiderate it was of my daughter and me not to attend! He pointed out that we were uninvited to the last party even though there was plenty of room at the freakin' bouncy house and even though they didn't even like half of the parents who attended. A little footnote to this story: a few months later, the stepdaugh-ter who gave me the mercy invite texted and asked what

I wanted for Christmas. I said, 'Kindness is free. Save your money.'" —Lakisha

Way back at the beginning of this book, we wished you a Happy Mother's Day, because we imagined you probably hadn't heard the sentiment from your stepkids and in anticipation of the fact that you may not hear it in the future. The stepkids may not have remembered your birthday, even though you've called them not only on their birthdays, but also on their first days of school, graduations, etc. But let's give them the benefit of the doubt and say that they've *forgotten*.

Unfortunately, the added complication in your stepkids forgetting *you* is that they often neglect *your kids* (their step or half siblings) as well, which is more heartbreaking than the omission of that damned Mother's Day card. But hey, kids will be kids, and your own bio kids might forget the same, which is a note worth remembering. It's never a bad thing to give a small, gentle reminder. How about starting with, "Hey, guys, it's your brother's birthday on Saturday. How about you make him a card (forget the gift)?" And then you've at least made the effort. Remind, remind, remind. And tell your partner to remind them as well. You may reach a point at which your reminders actually sink in…or not. But at least you've tried, so when your fourth grader says to you, "Why didn't my brother remember my birthday?" you'll have had the time to figure out a convincing reply, or you'll just keep to the truth and say, "Well, kids are sometimes really bad at being considerate." And then you let go and say to yourself, "Not my circus, not my monkeys," because there's nothing more that you can do.

You heard it here. It may not happen to you, but it happened to us, and we just want you to be prepared.

Life goes on. That's an important thing to keep in mind after each decision you make—the good ones as well as the ones that inadvertently turn out to be not so good. If families are complicated by their very nature, then stepfamilies are like having complications in the operating room during gall bladder surgery, in a raging storm, without electricity, under water, on Mars. You should know that.

TAKEAWAYS

- Take charge. Make sure you're listed as a contact for your stepkids and that you are included on the information chain.
- Don't try to do it all or be everything to everyone. Don't feel compelled to go to every activity and event your stepkids are involved in. Figure out what works for you, and easy does it!
- Have "quality time" as a family and individually with each child.

- It's okay, we repeat, *it's okay*, for you not to feel the same way about your stepkids as you do about your bio kids. Just don't say it aloud.
- Make dinner time a family ritual…with and without the stepkids.
- Blending (mashing/dicing/splicing) your families takes time. Everyone is experiencing change. Be patient. Only through trial and error will you find a working model for *your* particular family.
- Delegate gift buying for the ex to Dad, if possible. And don't expect cards and gifts from the stepkids. All together now: no expectations.
- Anticipate your stepkids' regular reentry into your home to be a bumpy one. Combat it with a plan—pizza night, family movie night, etc.
- Expect to be overwhelmed and unappreciated. It's your new norm, at least in the beginning.
- Send polite regrets to that "special event," instead of braving a potentially unpleasant or volatile situation. There, you have permission.
- Sometimes you just have to throw up your hands and *let it go*, whatever *it* may be. Remember, "Not my circus, not my monkeys."

CHAPTER 6

The Ex-Wife/Girlfriend/Spouse

(a.k.a. the Stepkids' Mom)

VOLUMES HAVE BEEN WRITTEN ON THE TOPIC OF "THE EX"
alone. Who is she, right? Who is the woman who was your
partner's wife or significant other before you, and why does
she have to be part of your life? The real drag is that if not for
children, his children with *her*, you would have very little reason
to have anything to do with her. But there she is, the mother of his
children, his children who may look like her, talk like her, walk like
her, and be a constant reminder of *her*. You may not know her, or
you may not want to know her, and you probably don't want her
in your life any more than you want your partner's twelfth grade
prom date, but she's there, and we're telling you right now that
you can take it. We know you can.

It's not just the children who benefit if you can maintain
some kind of civil relationship with the ex; it's you and your partner
as well. Yes, you! The odds are pretty slim that you are going to be
the one in, oh, let's say, a gazillion (rough estimate, of course) who
gets along famously with the ex. It's probably not going to happen

(and if it's happening now, it could turn in a heartbeat—be wary). The best you can hope for is civility, which means putting differences, resentment, and anger aside for the sake of your entire new family, not just the kids. What does that mean in terms of nuts and bolts? Just for starters, we've compiled the following list.

What Not to Do in Front of Your Stepkids

- Never say anything bad about their mother. Doesn't matter if she's Attila the Hun—she's *their* Attila. Remember what it was like trying to convince someone from an opposing party to vote for your candidate? Right? Like hitting your head against the wall before having Joe Pesci smash it in a vice. Remember, blood binds (usually), and loyalty is first to Mom.

- Don't discuss custody and money issues in front of the kids. This includes support payments, alimony, and the discrepancy you and your partner are having with his ex over the two-thousand-dollar veterinarian bill to save the kids' seven-year-old hamster. Don't do it, even if the hamster died. Don't have the money discussion in front of the kids.

- Don't talk about how you were responsible and thoughtful enough to attend the kids' play/game/ graduation even though Mom didn't make it. Keep quiet. The kids know Mom missed it, and you bringing it up will just make them feel badly. Your silence is way more important in terms of supporting them and showing that you care.

- If your stepkids want to talk about some disappointment with their mom, just listen. No need to chime in with "Now you see what kind of s*** I've had to face in dealing with your crazy mother!" Nope. Negativity on your part will always come back and kick you in the teeth. Mom will apologize to them, and then they will forgive her, and then they will tell her exactly what you said.

"When my husband and I were first married, the ex-wife insisted that we meet at their therapist's office to do the parental exchange for his eight-year-old son. After about six months, she started driving him to our house, where she would sit in the driveway for hours, 'talking.' Who knows what kind of stories she was telling him? I finally stopped pausing my life in waiting for her to release him from the car. When he'd eventually come to the door, I would act completely nonchalant, and I'd calmly welcome him." —Syd

Looking Through the Ex's Eyes

Okay, so you're biting your tongue (if that's what it takes) with what you say about the ex in front of the kids. What about dealing with the ex directly? Maybe you're still secretly fantasizing that you will be the heroine of your own Disney movie by magically stepping in to resolve all disputes between your partner and his ex, all for the sake of the kids. If your partner is having such a difficult time of communicating with her, you, in your passion and zeal and general zest for life, may imagine that you will not only embrace the kids, but you will also find it in you to embrace their mother as well. Okay, take a breath, and rethink this one.

"I leave all the communication between the exes to the exes! It's their parenting plan, and if they have a dispute, then they can go to mediation. I try to stay out of all their drama, which is extremely diffi-cult to say the least. I've learned that when I express dissatisfaction in the way a situation is playing out, my husband is already a step ahead of me. He sees what's happening. He knows, but he also knows that there's usually nothing he can do to appease his ex. I stay out of the way so that at least I'm not pulled into the drama. Then I can be present for my husband and my family." —Elizabeth

---

Take a quick look at your situation through the ex's eyes. No matter how good a person you are, no matter how pure your intentions, there is most certainly anger, guilt, and definitely a big fat dose of disappointment in having failed at a marriage, perhaps on the parts of both the ex *and* your partner. Add children to the mix, and you compound the fear factor in the ex—she may feel as if she's losing her kids' affections to another woman, even though you have no intention of replacing her.

No mother wants her children to love another mother figure more than her. Now take into consideration that your partner is on the mend, obviously, because he has moved on by choosing to be with you. However, in the wake of his moving on to a new life, the ex may not have moved on. A healthy person will try and move on, but an unhealthy person will remain angry and manipulative until they burn down everything around them, including you and your new, complicated life. Even more astonishing is how many ex-wives continue to plot and scheme against their ex-husbands even after *their own* remarriages. We've seen it firsthand, in our marriages and in dozens of others, which is why we bring this up.

Look, we're writing from what we know, obviously, and we're writing so that we can help a woman who is either testing the waters of stepmotherhood or feeling like she's already drowning in a situation not of her making. Why, you may ask, are the stories so, well, so *crazy*? The stories are crazy because they are our stories and the ones told to us by the women we've met. There are relationships between stepmoms and bio moms that work and that are even enjoyable, but the truth is that you won't hear about them, *because* they *are* getting along, and because, quite frankly, those relationships are an anomaly in the world of blended families. Those mothers and stepmoms are probably getting along because of a shared *sanity*, if you will. What's left are these real stories of conflict and resolution that we hope will give you encouragement, if not a bit of fuel and a few strategies.

There Are No "Wins" (Not Really)

Just as you must learn to pick your battles with the kids and your partner, that advice goes double for the ex—for the sake of your sanity, your happiness, and your marriage. There's no *winning*—although sometimes you can actually feel the tinges of a victory, but that's a little like knowing you have an infinite number of soufflés to bake, and you suck at baking, but every, like, seventeenth soufflé actually comes out as it should. Yeah, a small victory is a little like that, rare and satisfying, until the memory of it is erased by the next minor crisis or major fail.

> "Very early on, I realized that not only was my husband's ex-wife insane, but she had also taken my husband to the cleaners in terms of child support. She had one child, Tyler, with my husband, and she didn't work, so she had somehow finagled an inordinate amount of child support and alimony. She took trips, had cosmetic surgery, and bought her son expensive gifts at Christmas and on his birthday, while my husband and I worked full-time jobs and bypassed vacations in order to support us, my two sons from my previous marriage, and our two girls together. Mom's antics of not letting us know about specifics of my stepson's schedule and yanking us around at the last minute in terms of pickups and holidays and school events was ongoing. I told my husband that I had no time or interest in her particular brand of manipulation and antagonism, so I was *out*. Which meant that I wasn't going to be taking an active

role in Tyler's life. I welcomed him when he was with us, but it was up to my husband if he wanted to take it further. I then told Tyler that if he wanted his father and me (and his siblings) to be at an event of his, all he had to do was ask us himself. Period." —Hallie

---

There will always be *something*. There's no real solution in dealing with the ex, just an understanding of what situations can be avoided, how aggressions can be diverted, what your response ought to be (given the circumstances), how you will move forward without having your whole afternoon or day or week or *year* blackened by the cloud that is the ex, and how you can *be prepared*. In preparation, there is sanity.

"Finally, *finally*, we went back to court to figure out what was actual and what was implied in the custody agreement. Finally, after mad, last-minute scrambles to pick up stepkids who weren't where they were supposed to be, and after hours of lost time because the mom conveniently 'forgot' to tell us of changed plans, we went back to court. I know there are organizations devoted to this kind of stuff, along with the means of mediation, but we needed help ASAP. The shenanigans stopped pretty quickly afterward." —Sandy

In our circumstances, the collective exes were not only aggressive and unpleasant (a kinder word for hateful) while we were battling broken custody agreements and court orders, daily schedule upheavals, and broken promises; they were vindictive and uncompromising. That morass of upheavals included the ex ignoring the custody documents, refusing to drop off the stepkids at a designated place and time, and dismissing Dad's right of refusal (meaning that your partner accidentally finds out that his kids are with the grandparents during Mom's business trip instead of with him). The issues included the bio mom signing up her kids at completely new schools without Dad's approval—with the expectation that he pay the extra tuition—as well as her continual scheduling of parties and activities during Dad's scheduled time with the kids *without* his input. To make matters worse, our partners were not the most confrontational when it came to their exes. Imagine: a successful, strong, considerate, articulate man unable to deal with the mother of his child(ren), unable to make successful appeals, unable even to hear the sound of her voice—a man transformed into a cranky, withdrawn mess after a particularly unnerving encounter. At first, we countered our spouses' inabilities to deal with their exes by stepping in as their reasonable surrogates. We believed we could save the day and slay the dragon. We didn't. We couldn't.

You can't and won't slay the dragon either. So let go of that dream of having the perfect response or the magic solution. What works in one situation may not work in the next. Ultimately, you must work on keeping yourself centered and your marriage sound.

"I just didn't understand how a mother wouldn't put her kid's best interest at heart! My husband's ex pulled a fast one and sent his daughter to a different high school than the one she'd attended the year prior. She wanted her daughter to go to her alma mater. So not only did my husband have to pay (because it said in the court agreement that she had final say in school choice), but my stepdaughter was also anxiety-ridden about the move. She confided in me that she didn't want to go to a new school where she wouldn't know anyone. She didn't want to leave her friends or the sports teams she'd been involved in, but her mother wouldn't be moved. Sure enough, my stepdaughter soon showed signs of bulimia at the new school. Again, in confidence, she told me that the kids were mean, but she was afraid to confront her mother. As much as I disliked her mother, I volunteered to talk to her, but when I attempted to do so, she told me that I didn't know her daughter and that I should butt out. Okay. I went back to my stepdaughter and said, 'Honey, I spoke to your mom, and now she knows how you feel and what's going on with you. The door is open for you to speak with her further.' Then I told my husband that I would *never again* speak with his ex." —Delia

---

Mom is controlling the kids? Mom doesn't view your inclusion of *her* child(ren) as generous and loving (because, come on, who doesn't want their kid to be loved?)? Mom is angry with you, even though you had nothing to do with the demise of her marriage to your partner? Yes, yes, and yes? Well, there's nothing you can do about *her* feelings. Don't take ten years to figure this out. Be at peace with all of that. Yes, it's stressful in the beginning when you're trying to figure it all out. We're certainly not telling you *not* to figure out the schedules and holidays and schlepping and alternate weekends. Yes, do all that to the best of your ability and to the best of what your particular situation will allow, but don't expect to alter another woman's feelings about who you are. Don't make your life about that. Do what you can, and let go of the rest.

"My partner and I decided that for too long, we put his kids first to the detriment of our daughter. Every other Chanukah, his kids were supposed to be at our house before the 5:00 p.m. sunset so we could light the candles at 7:00 with our daughter (a tradition she looked forward to all year). Invariably, the ex would drop off my stepkids an hour or two later than 7:00, which would ruin the evening for our daughter. If my partner and I told his kids (and the ex) that we were picking them up at 5:30 for a baseball game, the ex would conveniently be out late with the kids or do something to avoid having them ready. Again, invariably, we would miss the first few innings of the game. We realized that our daughter was being treated like the child of divorced parents! We finally agreed that the world couldn't stop for his kids. We now light the candles at 7:00, whether his kids are at our house or not. If they're not ready to be picked up at the agreed-upon time, then we head to the stadium without them. Everyone in the family deserves respect." —Ashley

Like we hit on in chapter five, there are actually ways to communicate somewhat indirectly with the ex, especially when the stepkids are in elementary school and junior high—the time when parents are continuously involved in their kids' after-school activities, fund-raisers, sports, and social clubs. If the ex isn't very good at "sharing," then go ahead and take the lead. Make sure your partner is introduced to his children's teachers, coaches, and instructors so that they feel comfortable calling or emailing Dad. Go ahead and help make this happen by writing the emails for him if you want (or must). You can help make sure that the people in your stepkids' lives know that the kids have an involved father as well as a (fill in the blank: vindictive, helicopter, overbearing) mother. It's okay to get to know the other parents of the kids your stepchildren interact with on teams and clubs. Most likely, you'll encounter another parent who understands and empathizes with your situation. Swing a cat by the tail, and you'll hit a stepmom, what with today's statistics. Staying in the loop will help prevent your life and schedule from being turned upside down at a moment's notice.

"My husband's ex was constantly pulling stunts that caused me to spend hours in tailspins and guessing games after school. I'd have it on our schedule that both stepkids needed picking up, and I was to get them and take my stepdaughter to a rehearsal and my stepson to a playdate a half hour later. I'd arrive at school to find that the mom had picked up her son and taken him home with her because she thought since the playdate was later, she could have some quality time with him. The message she'd leave with my stepdaughter was that I had to drive to Mom's house to pick up her son (which was twenty-five minutes in the opposite direction), so of course, that left me scrambling to get to two places in half the time I'd allotted. After a few of these type of 'mix-ups' (that was the term the mom used), I photocopied a calendar of the pickup schedule and gave one to the ex and one each to my stepdaughter and stepson. Then I got my husband on board to tell his ex that if she pulled any more 'pickup' stunts that we'd be calling the police and would give evidence of her violating the parental agreement. I just didn't have time for that crap." —Ella

If your situation is particularly heated—meaning that the ex tries to undermine and sabotage your involvement at every juncture—but you still insist on remaining involved in the stepkids' activities, and, in fact, your stepkids appreciate your involvement, then encourage your partner to bring in the big guns. In the most simple and calm way, your partner needs to let the administrators, coaches, counselors, teachers, crossing guards (you name it; everyone involved in the stepkids' lives) know that the kids are from a divorced family and communication with the ex is extremely difficult, if not contentious, in which case all notifications for activities need to be signed or approved by *both* parents—Dad and Mom.

In order for this to work, though, parents need to have joint custody. However, even in a case of joint custody, never assume that Mom is sharing any information. If holiday custody is spelled out in an odd/even schedule—say, odd years she gets final say, and even years your partner does—never assume that even though the ex *says* she has no plans and that Dad can have the kids on her year, and you have gone so far as to book a holiday vacation and *tell her* about it, she will not pull a last-minute switcheroo. You can book all the tickets you want, as far in advance as you like, but unless it's in the custody agreement for you and your partner to have the kids on a particular holiday, Mom can pull a fast one.

"For me, there were more than a couple of straws in that proverbial bag of 'last' ones, but the biggest was a trip we had planned with my daughter and my husband's stepkids: a trip to the Bahamas that we'd spent months planning (booking tickets and travel arrangements) and telling the kids about. Somewhere along the line, the stepkids told their mother, and due to some glitch or misunderstanding *in the custody agreement*, she called a week before we were leaving to tell us that she was taking her kids on a vacation during the same time. To grind salt in the wound, she was even taking them to the same town in the Bahamas. There was nothing to be done at the time. My husband and I and our daughter went anyway, although she was disappointed that her siblings weren't there. But that was *it* for me. I told my husband that the parenting plan had to be fixed, that he had to take his wife back to court, or I would leave with our daughter." —Loretta

As in debates and criminal trials, stay on topic if it falls on you to figure out details having to do with the kids (and isn't that really the only reason why you would need or want to deal with the ex?). Walk away from her if she brings up anything that doesn't have to do with the kids. If need be, write yourself a little script in advance. Know what it is you need to discuss, and keep the conversation simple and focused. Fortunately, in our email- and text-centric world, other than during the time of *exchanging* the kids from one house to another, there ought to be very little reason to have conversations in person with your partner's ex. Think of yourself as being in a business situation—you're polite, organized, and appropriately impersonal (which translates into not taking *personally* anything she may sling at you).

Remember, she's *his* ex, not yours, and quite honestly, in a perfect world, *he* should be dealing with her, not *you*. (Hey, that's only our perfect world, and we can dream, can't we?) Though the truth of the matter is that those of us who made the most attempts at "meaningful" conversations with the ex (in the dashed hopes of improved communication and civility) suffered through the most blatant lapses in our own *sanity*. The stepmoms who could count on one hand the number of extensive conversations they'd had with the ex remained sanest (at least in regard to dealings with the ex).

Bottom line: it is absolutely okay not to have contact with your partner's ex other than polite, superficial pleasantries (if you can even manage that). Remember one of our favorite mantras: not my circus, not my monkeys.

"I know there's nothing to worry about when I have to see the ex, but I still get so anxious. She was so invasive and mean for the first three years of my marriage that I had to be on antianxiety medicine every time I knew we were going to be at the same social function. Eventually, I got into TM (transcendental meditation) and biofeedback and was able to cope with our scheduled and 'accidental' meetings (we live in the same town). I was able to gain relief from recognizing her real psychological deficits and how fortunate I was in my relative sanity. I couldn't change her, so I worked on myself." —Michaela

---

"I no longer get involved in my husband's drama with his ex. I no longer listen to every detail or ask questions beyond what I need to know about dealing with the kids. I'm involved with the kids, and I'm helpful, but I realized that I didn't need to know the nitty-gritty details of every conversation and email exchange with the ex. If I had anything to do over, I would have realized this from the beginning of my marriage instead of waiting until I reached the end of my rope after thirteen years." —Kim

It's such an exhausting challenge dealing with a mother who acts, on her best days, like her own tyrannical ten-year-old (talk about modeling crappy behavior). When that is how the ex behaves, view it as a perfect example of what not to do. Even in the worst of situations, despite lies and deceit and game playing, you have to remain focused on your own happiness and that of your marriage and your family. You can't manage it all, so don't even try. Say no to "fixing."

"When my stepkids are with us, my partner starts to get texts from his wife at 6:00 a.m. The texting lasts until midnight sometimes. Stupid stuff, mostly. He asked her via email (always keep a record of conversations!) to please keep the texting between 8:00 a.m. until 6:00 p.m. She didn't listen, so now he ignores her calls and texts during those hours. I do as well!" —Floria

Avoid the fantasy of thinking that if you could only find the *right words* to say to everyone and do the *one right thing*, all the anger and resentment between you and the ex, between the ex and your partner, and between the stepkids and you will melt away. Forget it! That's the "before" story, book one in the series, and there's no rewriting it. Get on to book two, the book that is your new family's story, and realize that it will take a lot of trial and error to write this book. No going back to book one. It's written. It's done. It's out in the world. Now it's about you and this new family of yours.

> "When my husband and our two kids were very young, toddler age, my stepson got involved in baseball. He was in middle school, and his father and I wanted to show our support, even though his mother would be there (she and my husband had no relationship other than via email). At his third game, the umpire made what my stepson judged to be a bad call, so he walked off the field. My husband went to talk to his son but was interrupted by his ex screaming obscenities at him from the stand. That was it for me. I had two little kids of my own, and I wasn't going to subject them to that crazy woman. My husband was free to do as he wanted." —Mitzi

As we've said before, the best possible way to deal with the ex is to let your partner do the dirty dealings. That would be ideal. But often, for whatever reason (sordid or otherwise), that's not possible, so you must at least let your partner know, without accusations and recriminations (because who in their right mind responds well to either?), that you two are in this game together and that if you are responsible for his kids—if only for one night of the week—then you must have his support in setting limits and rules. It's up to your partner to back you up when Mom says that her perfect children need no rules or that the only person who can set such rules is, indeed, Mom. Well, Mom doesn't live at your house, and it's up to Dad to bring that home, even if it is for the 1,127th time. No matter how loudly Mom yells, you are not to jump. Again, in *your* home, *you* are not the outsider. Having the support and respect of your partner is key in dealing not only with the ex, but also with his kids and the whole carriage full of family and friends that came with him.

"The ex always manages to know exactly where to sit at all the kids' events...basketball games, school plays, choral recitals, communions, ballet performances. She'd always save seats for her and the grandparents (and half the people in town) but never for my partner and me and our children (her own children's half siblings!). My stepchildren would always look for us and feel very awkward in having to go back and forth between their mom's family and our family. So I asked my partner to tell his ex (*in front of their kids*) to please let us know in advance where to sit so that we can all be together for the children's sake. As painful as it was for me to deal with the ex (who I like to refer to as the rudest woman on the planet), the kids were all much happier with the arrangement. Evil ex-wife glares be damned!" —Meredith

---

"Thanksgiving breakfast was always a big deal to me, because it was a family tradition that dated back to my childhood. I vowed to continue the tradition when my daughter was born and include my stepson. Of course, since it was 'my' tradition, my husband's ex-wife made a huge fuss about those few morning hours. For the first several years, she proceeded to make my stepson feel guilty about spending Thanksgiving morning with his father, half sister, and me—mind you, we're only talking about the morning, not Thanksgiving dinner. For years, it was a tussle. The week leading up to Thanksgiving Day, my stepson and I would plan breakfast and bake cookies as part of the preparation. He was super excited about the new family tradition, but at the last minute, the ex-wife would whine to my husband about being lonely in the morning, and he would give in. Finally, I got so angry that I told my husband if he didn't back me up on this one thing that meant so much to me—after having his back 24/7—I would take our daughter to my parents' house across the country and continue the tradition with them. I told him he would be more than welcome to join me or stay put and acquiesce to his ex-wife's whims, but enough was enough. He finally heard me and stood up to the ex. My only regret is that I didn't give him that one ultimatum years sooner. It was a matter of my husband cutting out the emotional blackmail and making our family the priority!" —Deana

Time for Therapy...Again

There's the *T* word again. You didn't think we'd let you get by without once again bringing home the importance of therapy. Sure, you may have tried it in dealing with child issues, but what if what's brewing between you and the ex has become so toxic and overwhelming that you don't know where to turn? Again, it may be time to seek professional support from outside your family. Talking to someone who is impartial to both you and your partner's concerns can greatly benefit not only you and your family, but it also gives you the means to arm yourself in dealing with the ex in a manner that won't drive you to drink, literally!

"At the first therapy session with my husband, the therapist asked each of us, 'What do you want to get out of this?' My husband said, 'I don't want to fight about how much money goes to my ex-wife or any other issues related to her.' I answered, 'I want a healthy relationship with my husband. I want him to understand how all of this affects the daughter we have together.' It was the first clarity we'd had in our ongoing battle with the ex and her game playing." —Bernadette

---

If you need ammunition in convincing your partner that the two of you need professional guidance in dealing with his ex, reassure him that it's because you love him and because you only want your relationship to thrive! How can he argue with that? Avoid any accusatory methods—*It's your ex. You need to figure this out. It's your fault that she behaves so badly and gets away with murder!* Accusations and blame don't work. Ask yourself, "Do they work with me?"

The goal of therapy is a reckoning with the shenanigans of his ex, which will help you and your partner avoid her siren calls—much like Odysseus, who had to be tied to the mast of his ship in order to avoid the call of those dangerous creatures that lured sailors to their deaths. We're not necessarily saying you should think of your partner as Odysseus, with you as his trusted first mate and his ex as deadly muse of the underworld, but if it inspires you to seek help, go for it.

"I've been with my husband since my stepson, Anders, was two. It was very difficult in the beginning, partially because Anders was being raised by his mom, dad, and his dad's mother, his 'gramma,' and because I was 'only the girlfriend.' At first, my husband's ex didn't even want to hear my name, let alone see me, so I would be conveniently 'away' for drop-offs and pickups. Even though I was in love with my husband and loved his little boy, the pushback from Mom and Gramma was so difficult that I went away for a few weeks to decide if I could deal with the whole family package deal. I came back and made the decision to give love and not take things personally. We got married when Anders was three. Through therapy with my husband, we've come to terms with a lot of issues, and I can safely say that I have earned everyone's respect by not only giving love and space when necessary, but also never apologizing for my choices. I've been the most conservative caregiver of the four of us and thereby have become the voice of reason. I think that happened because Gramma just wants to see her grandkids happy, so she is the most accommodating (and spoiling), and Mom and Dad both still feel guilt—which is never-ending—about every wrong move they may have made or might make, and they worry about being the least favored parent. When they ask my opinion, I raise concerns they haven't considered. Sometimes they listen, and sometimes they don't, but I do believe that love and communication have brought about respect. They all know how much I love Anders." —Cora

Communication

We understand that between you, your partner and his ex, the kids, stepkids, extended family, etc., there's a veritable cauldron of emotions brewing constantly. What we've discovered in our combined years as stepmoms and what we've gleaned from the dozens upon dozens of stepmoms we've spoken with is that the number one problem in a second marriage stems from communication issues (which is putting it mildly) with the ex. Go ahead, call it communication, verbal dodgeball, word assault and battery, crazy-freakin'-surreal-not-making-sense arguments. Call it what you may, but the communication issues will emotionally wear you out faster than you can say, "I'm calling a lawyer!"

What you may want to keep in the back of your mind is the understanding that some of the ex's bad behavior may be stemming from the genuine fear that you will replace her in her kids' lives. Can you hear that? Every undermining move on her part may be caused by her fear that you will give her kid more attention/care/ candy—whatever—than she is able to give. And it's this fear that may feed into her lack of rules and her poisoning of the kids against you. It's not a good excuse (you know we're not making excuses for her), but it may be the truth. *You* know you're not trying to steal her kids or raise them in the perfect manner, but there's no communicating that to her.

Look, we know this knowledge may not make a difference in communication and co-parenting agreements, but just take a moment to let it in. It may give you a bit of perspective, if not an iota of understanding and (dare we say) forgiveness of the ex's notorious behavior (especially that one time at Thanksgiving when she...). And like we keep reminding you, we're on *your* stepmothering side. We've been there, so we know that sometimes (just sometimes) we fight just to fight, because we think winning is important, and we'll be damned if we let some other woman dictate our lives. That's when you must ask yourself why winning is so important for you. Who cares if the ex wins (sometimes)? We can even provide an answer for that: you're fighting her because of the very nature of her *control*—her control over your life. But why give her that power? If you let go of whatever point you're trying to win or make, if you loosen your pit bull jaw and release, if you let it go, you will win in a different, healthier way. You will win because all that energy of trying to win over the crazy ex can now go into something else, like your relationship with your partner or your kids or your work.

"I do all of the communicating with the ex regarding my partner's children, because whenever he spoke with her, there'd be an argument and nothing accomplished. Thank God for email and texts. However, I never know whether I'm going to be dealing with Dr. Jekyll or Mr. Hyde. I'm polite and calm. Sometimes she almost seems friendly, and I'll think, 'Wow, maybe we can actually communicate like civil adults.' But then she'll hit me up with a nasty email about how I did or didn't do something 'right.' You'd think that after seven years I'd learn, but I keep hoping for my stepdaughters' sakes that we will finally have some kind of cordial relationship." —Jessica

---

Ever hear of writing "the letter that will never be sent"? It's a trick that was told to us by someone who does exactly that when she is faced with a troublesome person in a no-win situation. She writes a letter to that person and then mails it in an unaddressed envelope—yup, just pops it old-school style into a mailbox with everything she's ever wanted to say (or yell) at said irksome person. It's her particular form of therapy, and in writing such a letter, she finds the clarity and, sometimes, the empathy and understanding she needs to move on. So, may we present to you a letter from the (maybe not-so-evil) stepmom to her partner's ex and bio mom of the stepkids.

Dear Bio Mom,

Please, listen.

Blended families are difficult, which means that we are both in this same difficult situation. It's my hope that we find and maintain some peace. I want to work with you, not against you, because I honestly care about your kids, so please know that what I'm about to say to you comes from a place of genuine goodwill.

- *I know, believe me, I know that you are my stepkids' mother, and I am not. I will never try to replace you. I can't. That said, I will honor your title and would appreciate if you would not refer to me as "the stepmom." It is dismissive and demeaning. I have a name, and it's not Stepmonster or Fake Mom or The Fill-In, either.*

- *When you treat me in a negative manner, you are teaching your kids that it's okay to be disrespectful. Eventually, they may believe it is okay to treat you (and others) in the same manner.*

- *Please don't brainwash your kids against me. It will have the same negative results as disrespecting me. Your kids will take on your negative behavior and be hurt by it.*

- *Please don't be rude to me during exchanges and when we meet at family functions or accidentally on the street. I will grant you the same courtesy.*

- *In fact, please encourage your kids to be respectful of my kids and me. I will do the same.*

- *I want you to be happy. I do. Please don't live forever in your anger about my being with your ex. It will cost you your health and happiness.*

- *I am truly sorry that your marriage didn't work out, but please don't make my life difficult because of it. My life is far from perfect as well.*

- *That said, despite what you may think of your ex, he is your kids' father. Please don't bad-mouth him. Let your kids make their own decisions about him. Trust that kids are very smart and observant.*

- *Please communicate with your ex so that we can best take care of your kids' needs. It's all about the kids. I know, for the most part, men suck at communication, so please feel free to communicate with me as well, as long as it is polite and respectful.*

- *If you are flexible regarding holidays and celebrations, I will certainly bend over backward to try and accommodate you in emergencies. And while we are on the subject of holidays and celebrations, let's try to keep the joy in those things, for the sake of the kids.*

- *It may not seem like a big deal, but please let your kids keep some clothes at our house so they feel at home here. It is stressful enough for them to pack every week in order to change houses.*

In exchange for all this, I can assure you that I will genuinely watch over your children when they are in my care. I will treat them with the same respect and love they offer me, which will benefit them as they move into adulthood. I promise. After all, don't we, as mothers (step or otherwise), just want our kids to be loved and feel love? What else is there?

Best,

The Stepmom

Alternately, now for something completely different.

A Letter from the (Maybe Not-So-Crazy) Ex-Wife to the Stepmom

Suppose, just suppose that the ex is not crazy. Suppose that we are giving her the benefit of the doubt. Better yet, suppose, for argument's sake, that *you* are the ex (and you may well be one, as well as a stepmom to your partner's kids). Let's take a moment to look at things from that perspective.

You've probably heard the old adage "Before you judge a

man, walk a mile in his shoes." It's a reminder that before you judge someone, you need to understand what they're going through. Basically, it's a call to empathy; in stepmoming terms, it means to put yourself in the position of the ex, at least theoretically. We'd like for you to take a little detour with us in said shoes, in order to perhaps gain some understanding of where the ex may be coming from.

Dear Stepmom,

I never imagined that after falling in love with my husband and having children with him, my marriage would end, and I would be sending my kids off to live part-time with him and his new partner. It makes no difference who ended the marriage, just that it wasn't meant to be forever. There's no use in assigning fault, as it will only cloud everyone's judgment and make this new chapter of our lives even more difficult than it needs to be. There are simply some things I'd like for you to hear.

- *A child can't have too much love. It may be difficult for me to share my child's love with you, but be patient. I do want to encourage and support my child's relationship with you.*
- *If my child says something negative about me, please don't feed into it by adding your negative two cents. I will do the same when the conversation on my end turns to you. Let's teach them together that mutual respect is important in any relationship.*

- *You and I will not be best friends, and that's okay. But let's at least try and have a working relationship.*

- *Please let my child's father discipline our children. It's not up to you to be the disciplinarian. Yes, I know, you demand respect, and you have household rules of your own, but I would expect that you never be aggressive with my children, verbally or physically.*

- *I can't know for sure what you may have heard through the grapevine about me. I don't care—better still, it doesn't matter. All that matters is my children's well-being, which, again, means not to feed into any negativity from my ex or his family or yours.*

- *If you want to take my child for a haircut, or buy a prom dress, or plan a graduation party—anything that may traditionally be something a mother might do—please take a moment to consider me, the biomom. Ask me for my permission or for my input, please.*

- *Please be as respectful of and sensitive to my children as you are to your own. Don't treat my kids as second-class citizens when they are with you and your bio kids.*

- *Further to the aforementioned: as long as you're praising your own kids for their accomplishments or good grades, praise mine as well.*

- *Ask my kids about their day, and please listen to them when I'm not around to do the same. If there is something important to be shared with me, their bio mom, please do so. Contact me. Share.*

- *Try to make my children feel at home when they're with you. This can translate into letting them decorate their rooms, choosing the snacks they like, asking them what foods they prefer. Let them help you shop or make dinner. Keep some of their favorite games, clothes, pajamas, shampoos, etc. at your place.*

- *If you buy my kids clothes, please don't ask them to change at your house and leave those clothes with you. Instead, ask me if I would please return them.*

- *I know that my children may be picky eaters. Please, within reason, let them have a say regarding meals—in the name of choosing battles.*

- *Please keep your opinion regarding child and spousal support to yourself. It is court ordered and is pretty much set in stone, at least for a while.*

- *As much as I want you to enjoy and respect, if not love, my children, remember, please, that you are not their mother.*

- *Regarding school functions, sports, and special events that include family, I'd appreciate a heads-up as to whether you and my ex will be attending. The fewer surprises, the better. Remember, our goal is to make the children feel as comfortable and happy as possible.*

- *Holidays. They're stressful with or without extended family. Please be sensitive to schedules and open to making adjustments so the children may enjoy their holidays. It often may feel as though they need to be in several places at once, and you and I know that is physically impossible.*

- *Cut me some slack. You may be in my shoes one day.*

Best,

The Bio Mom

TAKEAWAYS

- Never say anything negative about the ex in front of your stepkids. (However, it is highly recommended that you and your partner come up with a nickname for her, for use just between the two of you. A little humor never hurts.)
- There's no "end-all" solution to dealing with the ex, just the understanding of your particular circumstance and your own mode of preparation.
- Remember, the ex is *his* ex, not yours. Let your partner do the dirty work (when possible).
- Seek therapy. It's okay, especially if you've tried everything else and you're about to go bald from pulling your hair out.
- Imagine the perspective of the ex-wife/partner/ girlfriend. It may not be easy, but it will help. In fact, there's a good chance that you, yourself, could or might someday be an ex.

CHAPTER 7

Just the Two of You

"Six nights a week, I dream of date night, when the wine flows freely and no one is begging for Capri Suns and corn dogs. Enjoy yourselves and leave the guilt home." —Alyssa

REMEMBER THAT PERSON YOU MARRIED? THE ONE YOU LOVE and to whom you made what you hoped would be a lifetime commitment? Wow, you may be saying to yourself, that was a long, long, *long-ass* time ago. (Especially because you became a stepmom instantly the day you married—remember that as well?) You may be wondering: did I actually *say*, "for the rest of my life"? We weren't there, but we're pretty sure you did, or maybe you read from your own script and said something like, "I promise to share the toothbrush holder with you and deal with your lactose intolerance until death do us part."

Or maybe you've picked up this book because you are readying yourself to jump into a relationship with a person who has kids, and, smart lady, you've decided to do a little investigative research to see what may be in store for you. Brava! In either event, the point we want to make is that you mustn't put "nurture your relationship with your partner" at the bottom of any important to-do list.

> "In our house, we have Sunday night as date night and a standing babysitter at 6:30 p.m. We either go to dinner or to a movie—the movies are never crowded, and the restaurants are usually empty. It's nice to have time with your partner and to be reminded of why you married in the first place. Rule of thumb: no talk of the ex during these dates!" —Kendall

You made a promise (or you're about to make one), and as difficult as life can sometimes be, you need to remember that promise. Remember that your partner has been dealing with his children and negotiating with his ex for a helluva lot longer than you have, but also remember that he promised to love *you*. You and your love agreed to be partners, a team of two, which means partnering in the roughest of situations, which often includes [drum roll] that carriage full of *others*.

> "It was impossible for my family to blend peacefully. I don't mean for this to be negative. I simply want to warn other stepmoms not to go forth all starry-eyed and naive. Be kind and loving to your husband and his kids,

and if they don't respond, you must find a way to take care of your marriage and to find peace. Eventually, all the kids, yours and his, grow up and become adults with their own lives. Now that that's happened, my husband and I are buying a new house, and I've declared it a 'hate-free zone'—yeah, you might be able to tell that I had a difficult time with one of my stepkids—where anyone who doesn't like me (or my dogs, or my furniture, or anything else in my home) is not allowed." —Zoey

Put the Kids First?

Seriously, now. We like to refer to this one as the biggest, boldest lie of stepmothering (and mothering, period). Sure, sure, if the scenario comes up regarding you on some hypothetical train track and whether you would selflessly toss the kids off and save them first or save yourself, yeah, it'd be nice if you chose the kids, but we're not talking about that kind of proverbial sacrifice. We're talking about putting your marriage first and letting all the kids see what a healthy, supportive relationship looks like.

We're talking about you and your partner respecting and not undermining each other in front of the kids, therein providing an example for them to follow. Imagine that through the thoughtful, loving, respectful relationship with your partner, you are able to mirror a healthy, loving goal for *everyone* in your household, since the only other marriage the stepkids know firsthand is the one that ended in divorce. Without overdoing it to the point of distraction (or comic PDA) and with sensitivity to your stepkids' feelings, hold your partner's hand, sneak a kiss, and let the kids hear laughter between you two. Believe it or not, children are afraid they'll be witness to the ending of yet another marriage/relationship—which is why most "experts" believe that kids should not even meet their parents' boy/girlfriend until at least the six-month dating mark. Children can learn a lot about a healthy relationship from you and your partner, including how to argue in a way that doesn't escalate into something nasty and frightening.

And speaking of that healthy relationship between you and your partner, it will remain that way if you and your partner keep an open and honest communication on what's happening in your household and if you also take the time to focus on the two of you (if only for a date night or a conversation in the privacy of your bedroom…or the bathroom, depending on where you can hide out from the kids). Recognize what's at the heart of your marital strife when it first rears its angry head.

"It is so important to take time out to be alone with your partner. Get a babysitter, or bribe a friend or family member. You need time off from being a stepmom and from having to deal with any ex-wives! Maybe even take up a hobby or sport you can do with your partner. If someone had told me a dozen years ago I'd be playing golf with my partner as a means of relaxing, I'd have told them they were nuts, but that's exactly what we do when we have time together outside the house." —Monica

Date Night

Speaking of date night—a concept we wholeheartedly support—set aside a regular one. Right now, go ahead, mark it on your calendar, time alone with your partner—time to focus on just the two of you, time for the emotional (and physical) intimacy that brought you together in the first place. Remember that time? Yeah, think way back. It's somewhere there before extended families and too many shared holidays and school and work priorities. There it is. You remember it. So whether it's a late Friday night in the house with a bottle of wine after the kids have gone to sleep, a night at a local pizza joint, a fancy dinner at a place you haven't been in *years*, or a couple of hours holding hands at a movie, make the time. Hell, make it a date for a bath together with candles, a hula dance across the bedroom floor, or an hour with some great lingerie in a locked room *somewhere*.

Once you're on your date, don't you dare use it to talk about the ex! Don't let her into your relationship during this time (that would mean giving her the power over your marriage on a silver platter). Remember things that you and your partner used to talk about before the drill of the daily routines took over, things that brought you together and made you laugh. Also remember that this time together is *not* the time to vent. No venting allowed. Start out with an anecdote of something positive that's happened to you recently or something you read or saw that made you think of him. Start with a memory. Offer praise or affirmation of something he's doing or handling well. Show your support, and he will, in turn, offer his.

"I'm a pretty type A gal. I realized that sometimes when I'd get overwhelmed by the day-to-day logistics and emotional crap of kids and stepkids, I would cling even more to all the rules and consequences I'd set up, and of course, those same rules and consequences were less likely to be effective, which resulted in my taking it all out on my husband. I figured out that sometimes I had to let go of everything and step back and ask questions instead of going nuts. What this has meant for me is that I don't 'go after' my husband, which makes our relationship so much better. It's a relief." —Morgan

Remind Yourself

There will be no "perfect" married life, even if you've had one pictured in your head. This is true in first marriages as well as second or third ones. There will be speed bumps and potholes and long journeys during which you may run out of fuel, which is why you must remind yourself to make every effort to avoid feeling resentful. One of the best ways to do that is to put yourself in your partner's shoes. Honestly and wholeheartedly imagine yourself as your partner. What does he want? We'll tell you, even though we've never met him. He just wants peace, and he wants everyone to get along. He wants you to be his partner, his refuge, his lover, and his voice of reason. (Actually, sometimes he doesn't want to hear any voice of reason, yours or otherwise, but you get the gist.)

"One night, my partner and I were in particularly dark moods over something having to do with his ex and his kids. So as a surprise for him, I made dates for our kids to have sleepovers at a friend's house, and I cooked his favorite meal (I even picked up his fave dessert from the bake shop). I had a nice bottle of wine ready as well when he walked through the front door. The look on his face when he realized the effort that went into the night was worth it all. I put on music, and we enjoyed each other's company. We even had conversations that didn't have anything to do with kids or his ex. It's natural to get stressed out and angry occasionally. You tell me one person who doesn't! But that makes it all the more important not to hold any grudges, especially against your partner. Your time alone together is the time to press pause on all the stuff making you crazy." —Quinn

Your partner's response to all the stress between his ex and his kids may be to go on automatic pilot. He may be the last person in the world who would suggest marriage counseling. Confrontation might cause him to take cover in his own world (or man cave). For all these reasons and more, you must remind him that he is *more* than his relationships with the ex and his kids, and that the health of your relationship is one of the most (if not *the* most) important things in your life. Protect your relationship, and if that means seeking out professional help, you tell your partner that you're doing it for the sake of the two of you. Fight for your relationship. Do this by focusing on your marriage instead of what is pissing you off about him and the ex and his kids. Let him know that by taking care of himself and your relationship (and avoiding the manipulation of the kids and the ex), he is actually modeling to his children that self-care and loving partnerships are important and worthy of every effort.

What does this mean for you? Well—ho ho ho, ha ha ha—it means, of course, a happier, less crazy you!

"Thursday night is our designated date night, our quality time together. We would plan an activity: go bowling, see an exhibit at the museum, go for a walk at a nearby park, go shopping, catch a movie, grab a casual dinner. Three hours tops. We would put our young daughter to sleep, greet the babysitter, and be out of the house by eight and home by eleven! Our mission? To simply enjoy each other's company and ignore everything having to do with the day-to-day aggravation of scheduling, blending, and ex-wife nonsense. Truly, our weekly evenings out (usually) never fail to remind us of why we married in the first place!" —Leah

---

"Date night was recommended by our couples therapist. He said we needed to keep the relationship cemented between the two of us. He urged us to set parameters—no venting about wrecked schedules, missed appointments, or ex-wife drama! But there was one evening, after a particularly rough knock-down-drag-out argument I had with my partner over (what else?) his ex and her usual game playing, that I almost cancelled because I was so angry and frustrated. Instead, I insisted we do something completely different. It was around Halloween, and we wound up going to a haunted house where we got the crap scared out of us! By the time we exited the house, we were hugging each other so tightly and laughing so hard that I couldn't even remember what I'd been so angry with him about earlier." —Sarah

TAKEAWAYS

- Make your relationship with your partner a priority.
- Show your stepkids a loving relationship—meaning that relationship between you and your partner. PDA included.
- Communicate with your partner and let him know you need him to have your back.
- Date nights, activities, or hobbies pursued exclusively with your partner are a *must*. Spend quality time together, just the two of you, without venting or discussions of the ex and the stepkids.
- There is no "perfect" married life. There is only *your* married life. The feeding and care of that marriage is up to you and your partner.

CHAPTER 8

No Pity Party

(Self-Care and Maintenance)

"Some days are better than others. One day, I'm having a lovely one-on-one with my stepkid, and the next day, it's like they've been possessed by the devil. On those days, I follow the advice from one of the songs from *Frozen*: 'Turn your back and shut the door.' But one day, I quite literally slammed a door and broke the doorframe. Next time, I got in my car, slammed shut the door, and listened to the song on Spotify. Voilà!" —Katie

---

WE UNDERSTAND! WE'RE OF YOUR TRIBE, REMEMBER? We know. We've been there. We've done that. We've had our days when we crawled into bed and cried. We've had times when we questioned our sanity and accused our partners of *in*sanity. We've all thought of throwing in the towel and filing for divorce (or wondering: would emotional self-defense be accepted in a murder trial?). First off, no matter how bad your stepmom story is, there's a worse one out there, even though it doesn't seem possible in an anxiety-fraught moment of screaming at an ex in a parking lot after a day of calming her puking child. It may not seem like it could get worse after dinner with said child who says for the seventh time, "My mom hates you and says I don't have to do anything you say." (No, no, of course, this scenario is not at all autobiographical.)

Sometimes the end result is worth the angst you go through. Maybe you learn not to sweat profusely when you bump into your partner's ex at the market, or that sick child hugs you and says, "I love you—even though my mother hates you," or your stepchild presents you with a crayon drawing of her family, and (huzzah) you're in the picture. Yes, sometimes in the moment that your strength dissipates completely or you've run out of solutions (or expletives), the clouds part, and the sun is revealed.

And sometimes the rain just keeps on falling. Realistically, you know that there's sunshine *somewhere*, but you can't convince yourself of that. You're bruised, you're hormonal, and your partner—despite his support and sympathy—can't and doesn't understand what you're going through.

Take a Break to Preserve Your Sanity

It's time for a break, for your own personal time-out, so to speak. It may be ten minutes of stepping away from the action (with a timer and instructions for *no one* to bother you) while you lock yourself in the bedroom (or even a *closet*) and breathe deeply. It's not about ignoring the pain and the disappointment (because at this point, if you try to ignore anything, you're going to explode). Rather it's about not staying in that house of pain. Recognize the difficulty of your immediate situation, and allow yourself some of the kindness you've been trying to dole out in generous offerings to *everyone else*. Cut yourself a big break, and forgive yourself for any mistakes. Stop beating yourself up.

"There were so many moments when I just couldn't help but feel sorry for myself—especially since my husband's ex so disliked me, and there seemed to be nothing I could do to change her feelings. I would remind myself that my husband loved me, and more important, I was a loving person! I realized I couldn't win by letting an awful situation get the best of me but that I did have to let myself experience my feelings. Sometimes I'd go to the gym or take a walk or simply take a time-out to cry, scream, or sit in silence. I'd 'release,' and then I'd regroup, with a smile on my face. I kept thinking that one day, the ex would like me, and all my problems would be solved. Well, it wasn't meant to be. I had to accept that she didn't like me, and there was nothing I could do to change her. I had to be okay with that fact in order to stop obsessing. It's life. Not everyone is going to like you...even if you are in the same 'family.'" —Jasmine

---

Preserve your sanity, ladies. It doesn't mean you're giving up; it means you're just taking care of yourself so you can return to that proverbial boxing ring of stepfamilyhood and roll up your sleeves and try again—with a new tactic or the same one in a different tone. You'll succeed...or you won't, but that's the never-ending process of life. Just show yourself the same kindness that you summon up for others.

"My stepdaughter is thirty years old, and she's as toxic as she was when she was fifteen. She's always been nasty to me, even though I've gotten along beautifully with her two younger siblings. She's simply rotten, but she's always had my husband wrapped around her little finger, and he's always come through with time and money for her—he's still paying for her car repairs and phone upgrades. Truth is, she's still angry with her father for leaving her mother twenty-five years ago. I've learned to say my piece, whatever that may be, in the most dispassionate way possible, and go on my merry way without letting his daughter 'rent space in my head.'

I've also learned that as strong and compassionate as my husband is, he is ill equipped in dealing with a daughter who will never forgive him and will always take advantage of him. Ultimately, I've learned to take care of myself and to find my go-to happy songs (I'll never get sick of Pharrell Williams's 'Happy' or anything from *Pitch Perfect*). I put them on in my car and take a drive. I go for a long walk in the park with my dogs. I see a good friend and bitch until I laugh. I take a long nap with my favorite spa candle. I allow myself amnesia of the unpleasant. I've learned." —Lynn

"After six and a half years of marriage and stepmother-hood, I finally decided to make time for myself. I realized I was so busy taking care of everyone else's needs that I had no idea what my own needs were. I needed to find an outlet or become an alcoholic (seriously). I decided to attend a yoga class one night a week. Best decision I ever made...an hour and a half of uninterrupted 'me' time away from everyone who 'needs' something from me." —Barbara

Need a few ways of finding the sanity, taking your time-out, redirecting your anger and anxiety, or just gifting yourself a little kindness? We've compiled a few things that have worked for us and other stepmoms. The bonus is that these are things that can help in any sort of stressful or frustrating life situation.

- Find a space in your home that is just yours. If that is virtually impossible, have a place that you can go to and be relatively by yourself—a favorite coffee shop or park—or take a long car ride by yourself with your favorite soundtrack.
- Speaking of soundtracks, find a happy one, a playlist that lifts you up and takes you out of the loop in your head.
- Choose a hobby or learn the thing you've always wanted to learn. Redirect your anxious energy. That new endeavor will be your go-to, whether it's making pottery, learning Italian or hip-hop dancing, or rolling the perfect tuna maki.
- Try not to take shit so personally. Ask yourself: Is the problem yours? Have you ultimately nothing to do with the problem? Meditate on finding the positive in a situation, which leads us to the next option…
- Take up meditation. Or yoga. Or kickboxing. Whatever your particular temperament demands.

Is it better for you to envision being shrouded in a gold light, or do you feel a thousand percent better after knocking something over (maybe consider the martial art of Krav Maga).

- Find the things in your life to be grateful for. Focus on them. Say them aloud, with love.
- Choose a friend or two who will be your first line of defense. You must know another stepmom. If not, find one. Text her. Meet her for coffee. Meet for a drink (more on this most important step next).

The Final Step Toward Sanity...Your Own Stepmoms' Club

"My stepmom group has truly saved my sanity. Sometimes the issue revolves around something insane done or said by the ex, and sometimes it's an issue involving her kids and/or angry, hurtful words. It's the ladies in my group who have pulled me off the ledge. They've not only provided constructive advice on how to handle a situation, but they've also let me vent like a crazy woman. We've got our go-to wine bar where any one of us will meet a fellow stepmom in need. Sometimes a quick

one-on-one turns into a powwow of four or five, and a
'talk off the ledge' turns into a raucous laugh-fest aided
by a bottle or two of Chardonnay. No matter. I always feel
better after I talk to these women." —Cameron

It's time to look for the support that lies with other women who
understand exactly what you're going through. Sure, by all means,
seek out therapy, with and/or without your partner. We wholeheartedly encourage you to do so, as professional help has provided
many of us with lifelines. But what we're talking about here, right
now, is simply that you must find your people, those women who
know what you're talking about when you say, "Who am I? I mean,
I'm not the mom, and I'm not the friend or the aunt or the sister
of my stepkids. So who am I, and what the hell do I do about [fill
in the blank]?" These women you go to, they are in the same leaky
stepmothering boat. Find them. They will provide you with the
empathy, understanding, and sometimes, the tough love you need
to get you through this Stepland (where few remain unscathed
and only the strong survive—okay, so maybe we're getting a bit
melodramatic, but you get the picture).

"One afternoon a few years ago, after my husband and
I had made plans to take all the kids (his two with his
ex and our two daughters) to a pumpkin patch, I heard

him on the phone arguing with his ex. Of course, I knew right away that she was demanding a schedule change (for the millionth time), which would blow our plans for a family trip to the pumpkin patch. I was really invested in the trip, because I thought it an opportunity not only to share some quality time as a family, but also to take a holiday card picture. Still, as usual, my husband gave in. I was left fuming mad and disgusted by his inability, once again, to stand up to her selfish, last-minute demands. I called two of my stepmom friends and left voicemails saying, 'SOS! Need advice. Have *had* it. I'll be at [our place] after work at 5:30.' My distress call was answered with the text: 'Will be there first. What's your drink pref?' After meeting and giving them a recap of the situation, they calmed me down and even made me laugh. Pretty soon, we were talking about everything else in our lives. They even convinced me to go to the pumpkin patch as planned. They insisted I be firm with my husband about going with our two girls, even if the stepkids couldn't make it. We went and had a great time—and I got some cute pictures of my daughters. I learned to go ahead with plans, *with* or *without* the stepkids, which sent the message to our kids that we were indeed a family by ourselves." —Janet

Look, whether or not you're a stepmom, you sometimes just need the company and support of girlfriends, but in the case of being a stepmom, the *only* people who you can (or should) talk to about your blended family issues are other stepmoms. No one who hasn't walked the step walk will fully understand what you're struggling with. The angst and anger, the game playing, and every emotionally charged step situation will be recognizable only to another stepmom. Find your step support group. Pull one together yourself. By turning to friends in similar situations, you can lessen the emotional burden on yourself and on your marriage. With a little luck, you'll see the forest for the trees and realize that a little perspective (and Cabernet) can go a long, long way.

"I met Kendall when our children were in a playgroup and she invited me to dinner with some other women. As it turned out, we were all stepmoms. I remember thinking, 'Boy, we are all intelligent women at the top of our fields. Why are we so successful at work but can't get a handle on this stepparenting business?' I shed so many tears being a stepmom. For so long, I gave up who I was and forgot to focus on what made me happy. Now when things are tough, I reach out to my group and text, 'Who wants to get a mani-pedi?' Our code words. Having the women of my stepmom group in my life is so important to me. Whatever the issues, I always feel better after we get together." —Cece

---

"It's crazy. I mean, I was completely naive. I thought I was marrying a man with two children. It never occurred to me that I was getting a family overnight. I soon realized that when his kids were at our house, I had to be their mother as well. There were so many times in the beginning when all I felt like was an unpaid nanny. My stepmoms' club helped me to deal with my partner's ex-wife, who was the biggest emotional and financial drain on my family. Talking to them provided break-throughs that gave me back my sanity." —Samantha

---

"My group of stepmom friends allows me to express myself regarding my partner's ex in all the ways that I would normally be ashamed of. I know I sound catty, vengeful, jealous, snippy, and downright nasty when I'm unloading about the ex-wife. My friends listen, and in their listening, I come back into the good side of myself. It's only then I can hear and understand their advice and perspectives on whatever I'm going through. Thank God for those ladies and our weekly (semimonthly or emergency) bull sessions at the local wine bar." —Dede

Last word on keeping sane and trusting in your girlfriends: it may be time to be your own best girlfriend. It may be a good time to ask yourself that sage question of the ages: Is this fight, whatever it may be, worth fighting? Do I really care? Have I chosen too many battles, and is it now fully depleting me? We know, we know, it's a tough one to answer, because you're just trying to do the right thing, but the truth is that maybe, just maybe, you're done. Hard as it may be, because, as we've pointed out, we women are naturally nurturers, it's time to turn off caring about whatever problem is eating you alive. It's time to stop giving a shit about the issue at hand, which leads us, finally, into *hitting the proverbial wall*.

"For a long time, the other women in the stepmoms' club coached and encouraged me to be less emotionally involved with my stepchildren, detach myself from the games that my husband's ex-wife plays, and withdraw from the drama between my husband and her. They were right, and had I followed their advice earlier, I would have saved myself six years of aggravation, stress, tension, and tears. As a stepmom, you are placed in an impossible situation. You can't win the game when everyone around you—your children, your stepchildren, your husband, and his ex-wife—are playing by different rules. Once I disentangled myself from the drama, it was so liberating. I felt as if a weight had been lifted from my shoulders. I should have listened to the women in my group." —Leslie

---

Hitting the proverbial wall is painful, but there is peace on the other side, believe us, because hitting the wall is cause for some big-ass reflection and a turning of focus on yourself, your own child, and your relationship with your partner. It's a time for looking through a different lens and tossing that two-hundred-fifty-pound gorilla off your shoulder. It may be frightening at first, but it is ultimately the most liberating thing you can do.

TAKEAWAYS

- Take a break. A personal time-out is imperative!
- Don't lose yourself in trying to keep up your new family. Don't forget what brings *you* joy, whether it's a particular sport or hobby or time spent curled up in a corner with a good book (or a cheesy, thrilling, bad one).
- Take care of yourself emotionally, physically, and spiritually. You know what that means. Review our list!
- Disengage emotionally. You'll be set free when you do. (Again, you are not the mother.)

- Don't let yourself be consumed by your role as stepmom. You'll lose yourself and who you are in the process.
- Our biggie: Create your own stepmom club. It's so important to have other stepmoms to talk to. No one will understand what you're going through better than a fellow stepmom. No one.

CHAPTER 9

Hitting the Wall

YOU'VE TAKEN ALL THE ADVICE, READ THE CUSTODIAL PAPERS, sifted through the financial decree, benefitted from our own lessons, learned from our mistakes, been forewarned of certain unforeseen circumstances, and planned accordingly. You've found ways to take refuge from the ex-wife/stepkids/blended family drama. You've even taken up meditation, joined a yoga class, met with your stepmom friends religiously for enough coffee and wine to float the ark, but none of that is making a difference right now. Yes, you've tried the best you could, didn't give up, tried too hard, didn't stop believing (yeah, just like the song), pledged your love, bent over backward, and prayed to God/Goddess/Buddha/Mohammed/Jesus/Oprah/your spinning guru. Now it's time for us to welcome you to *here:* the point when you realize that although you've tried as hard as possible for as long as possible to make everyone "play nice" together, it will probably never happen. Probably. Never. You have, as we have learned to call it, *hit the wall*. It may sound painful and daunting, but wait...

Hitting the Wall Is Not Necessarily a Bad Thing

There is actually a joy in hitting the wall, a kind of liberation in the aftermath, because only upon hitting the wall do you truly gain acceptance of *what is*. It's only after hitting the wall that you realize that instead of struggling to change your circumstances or rewrite a history that you had no part of writing in the first place, you may let go of certain impossible expectations—expectations of what your relationship should be with your stepchild(ren) or what their relationship should be with your partner, or how you ought to sacrifice yourself and your needs for everyone else. It's the understanding that you don't have control of whatever it is that you believed you *could* control—your stepchild's unkindness, the ex's bad behavior, or your partner's unwillingness to recognize either of those things.

As much as you are not responsible for everyone else's happiness, you *are* responsible for recognizing that very same thing. Sometimes you have to hit the wall for that to happen.

"After eight years of planning family vacations by coordinating three different school schedules (between my husband's two children from his first marriage and the son we have together), allowing for custody schedules, making multiple calls to hotels and airlines, and having 'discussions' with everyone about the ideal vacation locale, I finally decided I was no longer going to be the travel agent. I relegated the task to my husband. I decided the juggling of his ex's schedule and that of his two high school kids along with confirming reservations during the craziest and most expensive vacation times of the year (Christmas and spring break) was not worth the aggravation anymore. Since our son was young enough to take out of school at 'off-season' times, I figured I'd at least plan little threesome adventures, and my husband could take care of the whole blended family vacation chaos. Sadly and ironically, a few months after my husband took over the planning, he gave up, and we never again had a blended family vacation. He didn't plan one, and I realized that if it wasn't important enough to him, it was not for me to be the super planner and make it happen. I struggled that first year, but then I put it out of my mind completely. We still have his kids for holidays, but the focus of our little vacation jaunts during the year are on my child, my husband, and our family time together." —Colleen

"My husband's ex made it extremely unpleasant to be at my sixth-grade stepson's sporting events, and he's a sports dude, so he had games in every season. At first, I wanted to be supportive, so I took my husband's and my young daughter to the games, but the ex would go out of her way to be rude to me and my daughter, which also made my ten-year-old stepdaughter very tense and uncomfortable. Ridiculous. I swear, at one basketball game, the ball landed in my lap, and I thought for a brief moment of hurling it at the ex's face. My daughter was aware of how badly the ex was behaving and how it was affecting one of her favorite people—the ex's daughter, my stepdaughter, her sister. After one particularly bad scene, I was done! I made the decision to no longer attend my stepson's games. It was important, though, to let him know that I wasn't ignoring him and that I would have enjoyed being there. I was advised by a therapist to tell him, 'Your mother gets very upset when I come to your games, aside from the fact that she isn't very nice to your younger sister. So as not to upset your mother, I'm not coming any more. I'd love to support you, but I don't like the way your mother acts when I'm there.' It was important for my stepson to know that it was his mother's behavior that caused me to make that decision." —Jessica

The moment may be here already, or it may come this afternoon, tomorrow, next week, or next year, but it will arrive at some juncture. You've begged your partner to act, you've tried to reason with his ex, you've bent over backward to engage your stepkids, but it's as though there is no record of any of your endeavors. In fact, it's as if all your efforts and good intentions have been deleted. The wall appeared out of nowhere in the path of your stepmom marathon. Sure, there were checkpoints along the road, hurdles jumped, progress made, but this one time is different. As we said, this proverbial hitting the wall moment is your wake-up call: *Hello, this is your life, too! Don't wake up another day to find out you've missed it! You can't fix what you didn't break! Move the hell on!* You realize that all the physical and psychological energy you've been expending to "make it all work out" can be put to better use.

No doubt about it; there are many different *tiers* of hitting the wall. The first tier may have to do with something as seemingly benign as "I'm done going to your nieces' birthday parties! No one even knows or cares if I'm there." Or "I'm not making breakfast at 6:00 a.m. any more!"

The top tier may involve the ultimate crash, the "I'm leaving you if you don't finally have my back and stand up to your lying ex!" or "If I'd known everything I know now, I never would have married you!" (Gasp.) It may be the first time you utter the *U* word (as in *ultimatum*, a final battle cry if there ever was one).

Whatever wall you're hitting and however hard you're hitting it, imagine that it is the opportunity for freedom, the chance to refocus your energy and break the loop in your head that's been playing, "I just gotta do this…if I only do this…if I could only think of the right words and deeds, everything would be perfect." There is no perfect, just as there are no right or magical words.

So you find yourself here. First of all, give yourself a much-needed pat on the back for coming as far as you have. Give yourself a break—a long, luxurious bath, a box of chocolates, a minute alone to stare into the trees. Congratulate yourself on your fierceness and your great effort and your loving nature, despite your feeling of helplessness in hitting that wall. Embrace it all, because after you've hit the proverbial wall, you invariably enter a period of *letting go*—a time when you take yourself out of a particular situation, mentally, physically, emotionally, and you reach for something higher, when you decide to *make the healthier choice for you*. YOU. Those words bear repeating: letting go is that moment when you recognize that there's something greater, when you realize that you must make the choice that is healthiest for yourself.

Here are stories of hitting the wall, presented to you so that you may avoid the same fate or recognize the source of your own concussion. (And if you think these are bad, we've heard worse—though try as we might, we couldn't get permission to retell those doozies.) They are our stories and those of the dozens of women we've talked to, and more than anything else, we've included them to convince you that you are not alone. For better or for worse, you are part of our club. We want to catch you before you utter those six desperate words: I wish I'd known this before!

We're letting you know.

"Fifteen years ago, when I met my husband, he'd just bought a new house, his first since his divorce several months earlier. His mother had decided to stop in and organize the new place, make his meals, and grocery shop for him. By the time I met her, she had basically laid claim to the house and even told me that it was inappropriate for me to leave clothes and a toothbrush there. My boyfriend (not yet my husband) told me to ignore her behavior. Easier said than done, because she was encouraging his daughters to be mean to me as well. She told them that my relationship with their father wouldn't last and that I was simply 'using' him. Between her, my boyfriend's ex-wife, his daughters, and his sister (who was best friends with his ex), I couldn't win, which only made me try harder and harder, which, in turn, caused me to take out my hurt feelings on my boyfriend. I realized that the things I loved about him—his kindness, gentleness, and need to please (well, I don't know if I loved that quality so much)—were the reasons why he didn't have the desire or energy to confront all those women in his life. I was the one who needed to disengage. My mother said to me, 'When you don't know what to do, do nothing at all.' And that's what I did. I stopped trying, stopped engaging. I became cordial but emotionally detached. I stopped overanalyzing the situation and stopped trying to fix it. After we married, things did get a little better, but only because I didn't give any of those women access to my emotions!" —Vita

---

"My husband was divorced from his first wife by the time his twin boys were one. He'd had a tumultuous relationship with his wife, as she was, I soon learned, certifiably crazy. We married when the twins were four, and since I'd been told by doctors that I had a 99.9 percent chance of not having children of my own, I was determined to create this perfect instant family. However, a year later, I got pregnant, which resulted in the birth of my daughter! I was not only over the moon about her arrival; I was so very invested in having one big happy family and raising all the kids as loving siblings. I tried in the beginning to have a relationship with the ex, but she crushed every overture I made and tried to foil my every attempt at including her kids in our family plans. In hindsight, I would have insisted in going through the parenting plan and working with a mediator to nail down the custody specifics from the get-go. My rabid investment in making a big blended, cohesive family gave me none of the returns I expected. It took years to learn that the ex had a greater choke hold on our family than any single one outside force. Finally, when my daughter was entering elementary school and she was catching on to the dynamic of the household, it hit me—or rather, I hit it. We had to be a family whether or not my stepkids were in the picture. I talked to my husband, and the two of us agreed that if his ex prevented his kids from being part of our family celebrations and outings, then we were enough as our family of three." —Grace

"My husband's ex had been in and out of his daughter's life, 'trying to find herself' for years, so I was thrust into the role of mom very quickly and intensely. The minute after we were married, my stepdaughter, who was eight at the time, came to live with us full time for six months. Afterward, we had fifty-fifty custody, but we often had my stepdaughter when her mother went on long, requisite business trips. I took it all on—sitting up with her all night when she was sick, doctor visits, class trips, and birthday parties—but truthfully, I really enjoyed doing it all, because I enjoyed my stepdaughter. I never tried to take her mother's place. Instead, I tried to accommodate the mother's schedule and her very needy personality. I know my stepdaughter was aware of how needy her own mother was, and I was the opposite. At my stepdaughter's high school graduation, my husband's ex planned the whole day without letting us in on anything. She whisked the grandparents in for pictures with the kid in her cap and gown, posed for a few herself, and then whisked her away. The ex intentionally made sure that there was *no* picture time with my husband or me. None. High school graduation came and went with not one photo memento. The ex didn't even have the decency to tell us that she was leaving. I realized then that Mom would always, always win, and that she would never stop trying to be 'the winner.' My stepmom friends learned from this that they must always, always find out the schedule in advance for every celebratory event. Know every detail down to the minute of departure and arrival. Take nothing for granted, even after *ten* years. And then, when you hit the wall, you'll realize you did everything you could, and you'll be able to let go and *not care*." —Kiley

---

It bears repeating here: the bio mom will always win out. Accept that fact. Deal with it and move on. Have you bent over backward for the stepkids as well? Doesn't make a difference. Ultimately, no matter what you do and how much love you pour into the doing, the stepkids may not give the same courtesy to *their* half siblings or stepsiblings that you give to them. Your stepkids may not treat your bio kids any better than they treat you. Once you realize this, you are released from making the kind of gargantuan, unappreciated efforts that led you smack into the wall in the first place. If we could wave a magic wand over you and rid you of the guilt of "letting go and not caring," we would.

Bibbidi-bobbidi-boo! There, we did it.

"Christmas is a big deal at our house, especially with four kids—two in high school and two in elementary school. One year, I also had my mother at my house. We all woke early as planned, raced down to the tree, turned on the lights, and waited. Yup, it was already half an hour past the time my stepson was to be dropped

off at our house, as per my husband's custody agreement. We all sat there, waiting. I don't think I have
to tell you how difficult it was to keep the kids from
ripping through their presents on Christmas morning.
We were waiting on Christmas, on breakfast, on the
festivities, because I wanted to include my husband's
son. Everyone was growing anxious, and I was on the
verge of losing it completely (for the first time I remember!). My mother, usually reticent to give me any advice,
finally turned to me about an hour in and said, 'What
are you doing? Why are you letting this woman hold the
whole family hostage?' A proverbial lightbulb went on
in my head. Of course! That's it. I'm done letting this kid
and his crazy mother rule our schedules and holidays!
We dug into the gifts and got our family celebration
underway. No more waiting on my husband's ex, no
more allowing her to control our entire family, which is
what we'd been allowing up until that morning." —Erica

It's so easy to get caught up in an endless back and forth of
accusations and fighting between the ex (and possibly her family),
your partner, and you, even when you're sure that everything
of importance has been worked out in the decree. Bio mom is
more often than not going to do whatever she wants, whenever

she wants. Sure, you can push back and try to create those sacred boundaries of yours (look, we know, we did it, too), but in the end, the ex will get her way. Please, trust us when we say that it's not worth the fight (nine out of ten times, anyway)—it's not worth the fight emotionally and financially and certainly not at the cost of your marriage. We understand that you at least have to try to make your case, try to win the battle and stand your ground. Absolutely, go ahead, do it, but don't get caught in the back and forth of a texting, calling, or email war. State your case. Make an effort, and then let it go. We've been there. We've done this, and we have the crazy stories and prescription antianxiety drugs to prove it. Like we've said: these are the things we wish we knew (say it along with us) before we said "I do." Corny, we know, but it drives the point home. Kind of like a mantra, don't you think?

"I get it. My husband has always felt very guilty about breaking up his family. He cheated on his ex (I met him years later), and one of his three kids never stopped punishing him for it. By the time I met my husband, his kids were teenagers, and the punishing one—I'll call her Ellen—was having dinner at our home for one of our first meals as a 'family.' After the meal, she told me that she hated what I'd cooked. When her father (my husband) told her that wasn't being very nice, she said to him, 'Suck my dick!' Well, my husband laughed it off (guilt does terrible things, ladies). I still tried to make our family work as a unit, believe me. Her two younger siblings were actually lovely, but Ellen...

Several years later, Ellen (then in her early twenties) was angry (yet again) with her father for some mild transgression. (I don't know...he wasn't available to see a certain movie or he didn't pay her phone bill...whatever.) I was supposed to go with my husband on a road trip to visit one of his other kids, but instead, I suggested that he bring Ellen. I thought it would be a nice way for them to have some father-daughter time. Fast-forward to my husband's return. Apparently, Ellen had spent the entire car ride telling my husband how much she hated me and that she never wanted to have a relationship with me. She even made up lies about me, lies that apparently went back several years, and my husband was questioning whether they were true. (Boy, she was really reaching.) For the first time, I went ballistic on my husband (I never yell) and said to him, 'She waited *years* to tell you all these stories about me? This from the same girl who can't keep a secret for a moment and who has apparently always hated me? And you believe her? You are completely blind to your daughter.' My husband paid for the guilt of breaking up his first family for years, and it made him overlook just what a bully Ellen was. My husband and I got as close as we'd ever come to divorcing, but I really do love my husband...he's a good, smart man. Instead, I said to him, 'I never asked you to choose between your daughter and me, but we are moving into a beautiful new home (that we were building together), and I insist that it be an Ellen-free zone. I don't know how to be mean, and I'm not going to start learning. Unless Ellen is dying, I don't want to know anything about her.'" —Tema

---

"I've been married to my husband, Richard, since his daughter, Leslie, was thirteen. Our son was born soon after. I've had a lovely relationship with Leslie, despite the ex-wife's spitefulness and constant mean-spirited attempts to thwart every holiday plan I've ever made. Okay, so she's horrible, but I think my relationship with Leslie has been successful because I've never tried to replace her mother. That doesn't mean that I wasn't on the receiving end of typical teenage angst and BS, but I was present (happily, mostly) for every ballet recital, cheerleading competition, graduation, and

parent-teacher conference. I lent support during friendship dramas, romantic breakups, and college visits...you
know, the whole 'through thick and thin' of it.

When Leslie got engaged, her mother very quickly
took control of the wedding plans—everything, even
though Richard was paying most of the cost of the
wedding. Leslie asked for our suggestions, but they
were completely ignored, less by Leslie than her mother
(since Leslie was never the type to make a big deal of
anything). My husband tried stepping in with his ex, but
it always ended in a screaming match. I felt hurt and
dismissed, because I really was invested in my family
being part of this special celebration. Well, my hit-the-
wall moment finally came when my stepdaughter and
her fiancé came by the house to share their excitement
about their beautifully printed invitations. The names of
her fiancé's parents were included, as were her mother
and father's names, but nowhere did it include me. I was
not even listed as 'Mrs.' or as 'Richard and his wife, Kate.'
No, no mention of me, after fifteen years of devoted
stepmotherhood. I was speechless as I grabbed my car
keys and went out the door. I got in my car, drove down
the street, and then pulled over and cried. I texted my
husband: 'There are no words for the hurt caused by

your ex and daughter. I'm going out for a drink with a girlfriend.' That was it. I decided I wouldn't even address the hurt with his daughter and especially not with the ex. I would go forward as a guest. I let go and became truly unconcerned as to whether my friends were invited or my son was in the wedding party. I was cordial and friendly and acted like any other guest. My focus going forward was on my son and husband. Looking in hindsight, it would have been great to sit down with all parties involved and make a mutual plan, but honestly, I also should have known that my stepdaughter never had the energy to fight her overbearing mother." —Kate

---

The worst of the hitting-the-wall stories, though, usually involves that God-awful sinking feeling of wondering if it isn't time to throw in the towel. You do love your partner, but you are seriously deliberating whether you can actually stay with him. Sure, you've had those moments of imagining what life would be like if you just picked up and left, but they were fleeting—a glass of wine with sympathetic friends and a good laugh or an hour or two of hitting a jogging trail (or punching bag—don't knock it until you've tried it) was enough to keep you on course and back in "the ring."

It may be that your partner feels too guilty (still, even after so many years away from his former marriage) to realize that his choice to placate everyone involved (*except you*) is killing your relationship. You experience that moment when the hurt is so overwhelming, you can't see straight, so *wham*, into the wall you go. However, despite the pain of the collision, what follows may be a moment of truth, a calm after the storm, and some peace from the chaos. And sometimes you do have to follow your instinct to leave before you can jump back in and repair the damage.

"I've always trusted my husband, Harry, on everything—everything except having my back when it came to his three daughters from his first marriage.

Early into my marriage to Harry, it became very clear that I could do nothing right by his daughters. They were angry with their father for leaving their mother, and he never ceased to function from a place of guilt, which invariably led him to believe that the girls could do no wrong. Since I had a daughter of my own, I needed to stay open and loving, if only for her and Harry. (Eventually, when the older two girls hit their twenties and began forging lives on their own, we were able to form a lovely relationship because they'd gained the maturity and hindsight to know I was not the devil, but I've no doubt the youngest would have had me boiled in oil.)

A few years into our marriage, Harry had snagged eight tickets to a much-anticipated ball game. However, four of the seats were up front and four were in the nosebleed section. The original plan included only Harry, my daughter, her friend, and me, but then Harry decided to invite his daughters. I said to him, 'Why don't you and your girls take the front seats, and I'll sit in the back with Sarah and two of her friends?' I then told his youngest that I was glad to give up my ticket so they could have some time together. She replied, 'Fuck off. They're my Dad's tickets in the first place.'

I will mention here that Harry had days earlier purchased a new smartphone that he had no idea how to operate properly.

Evening of the game, Harry, my daughter, her friend, and I arrived at the stadium in time to grab a quick dinner at one of the fast-food vendors inside. I offered to run ahead and get in line for food, so I asked Harry what he wanted to eat. Meanwhile, one of his daughters had apparently texted to ask him to join them for dinner in the clubhouse restaurant (entry came with the front-row tickets). Harry disappeared without a word to me. I called him just as he was sitting down to dinner with his daughters! He claimed he told me of his change in plans, but clearly, he hadn't. Worse yet, because he hadn't the guts to say no to his daughters, he dumped my daughter and me and tried to convince me that it was my misunderstanding. I was upset and told him so. Surrounded by his daughters, he said loudly into the phone, 'You're crazy' and then hung up—or he thought he hung up. He'd only placed the phone down, assuming he'd disconnected. I stayed on the open line, which is when I heard him say, 'She's crazy.' His daughters chimed in with the most awful garbage about me. The worst part was his laughter and tacit agreement—he was chiming in in order to please his girls. After listening to their twenty-minute verbal evisceration of me, I hung up and called him back. I said, 'You need to learn how to use your phone, because I heard everything you and the girls said.'

His reply? 'Oh, don't be a baby. You're making that up.'

I then went on to repeat, verbatim, everything I'd heard.

He had no defense, so instead, he said, 'Get over it. It's not a big deal.'

Well, it was more than a big deal; it was devastating. My friends had to pick me up off the floor. I went to my minister and told him I was done with my marriage and that I was leaving my husband. I did. I left—for several nights.

When I went back home, my husband admitted to me how torn he felt between his daughters and me. I said to him, 'I'm not doing the tearing. What you're feeling is guilt, and I'm not paying the price for your guilt. I can't be the target, no matter how much you think I can take.'

I told him that I loved him and then I asked him point-blank if he still loved me and whether he wanted to stay in our marriage. The answer was, thankfully, yes and yes, and after counseling, I was able to believe him!

It was a long process of healing. I understood that my husband was overcome with a shit storm of guilt, which he was too stubborn to recognize. I had harped and harped on the treatment I was receiving from his girls, Zelda in particular. In my life, I was used to bulldozing issues and writing follow-up letters to state my case, but I realized that in this marriage, with this particular person, my tactics weren't effective. I remember telling a friend, 'I bitch and bitch to Harry, but he doesn't seem to hear me.'

She said to me, 'That's because he's a man. Be quiet, and he will hear you.'

And so I did just that. I realized that Harry heard me best in my silence. I learned to state once what a particular problem was and then let him process my words without a constant barrage. If I couldn't say something aloud without rage, I'd write it down in a letter and move on.

Harry and I got through it all, and I can honestly say that our relationship has strengthened in time, but it hasn't been easy. It has, though, been worth it." —Rinko

---

Keep in mind the silver lining to hitting the wall (once you've nursed the psychological and emotional bruises and that crazy hungover feeling), that sense of clarity you gain, as though waking up from a bad dream. You're awake and back in your body with a renewed sense of yourself (at least until the next wall pops up in your periphery). It's as if a weight has been lifted, and you have that moment of seeing the proverbial forest. You're moving forward, and you frankly don't give a crap—right here and now—about a battle won or lost.

"I'd been divorced twelve years, and my only child was in college when I met Scott. He'd been divorced for several years, and he had two boys in middle school who were longtime (fanatical) soccer players. I mention this because

Scott was very involved in the boys' sports schedules *and* because the ex-wife was as well. In fact, it was her longtime affair with Scott's oldest boy's coach that precipitated their divorce. The whole situation not only became very public, but it was also so ugly that the boys had to switch to new teams. After the divorce and fifty-fifty custody was determined, Scott made sure that everyone under the sun knew he had joint custody. Because communication between him and his ex was very difficult, he also made sure to receive all schedules, memos, notifications, and text/email message chains regarding the boys' games. Even though he was always on top of the boys' needs—organizing car pools for games and practices, providing snacks—his ex-wife never ceased to text him on his custody days with endless messages of 'Did u drop kids at practice? R u picking them up? Did u remember snacks?' When he didn't respond, she'd send email/text chains to every parent on the team asking, 'Was Johnnie dropped off? Did he bring snacks? Scott isn't responding, so I need to know.'

After dating Scott for a long while and having met the boys, I was to attend the younger one's soccer game for the first time. Scott had prepared me. I knew that his ex loved to talk loudly about her and Scott's dirty laundry, and I also knew that my first encounter might wind up in a loud confrontation (on her part), so he and I agreed to a plan of defense ahead of time. I was determined to prevent a bad situation before it happened—before I hit a wall. As soon as his ex-wife caught sight of me, she went ballistic and said aloud to any parents within earshot, 'Who is that? What the fuck is she doing with my kids? Look at the way she's dressed.' And so on. Of course it was loud enough for me and Scott and his older son, who was sitting with us, to hear, even though we were at the opposite end of the bleachers. Honestly, as prepared as I was, I couldn't believe how inappropriately she was acting. I wanted to laugh. It was like listening to a bratty child.

During halftime, it was no accident that we all wound up at the snack bar area together—me, Scott, his older son, and the ex, who was still yapping loudly a few feet away about 'Scott's new girlfriend.' I went right up to her—mind you, she was surrounded by the other parents who she'd been haranguing—and I said, 'Hi, I'm Barb, as you already know, and I understand that you've been bad-mouthing me and Scott, which is odd, considering that you two have been divorced for years, and as you and everyone else on this team knows, I had nothing to do with your divorce. So here's the deal. I am going to be in Scott's and your sons' lives, so it's best if you act like a responsible adult for the sake of your kids. I'd be happy to sit down with you at any time, but I have no desire to put up with your bullshit, as Scott has been doing all these years. And if you don't believe me, then test me.'

The ex's jaw dropped. She looked around at everyone, including her son and Scott, then silently walked back to the soccer field. As she walked away, my future stepson high-fived me, and Scott gave me a quick kiss and a wink. Not a word was heard from the ex for the rest of the game. The bad behavior came to an end. Dragon slayed." —Barbara

So as a reminder, because we've said it before, but it's time to hear it again, fresh: pick your battles. It's a directive that applies to every crazy, ongoing situation in life, but in stepparenting, it means that if the ex or the stepkids or anyone else is holding your family hostage with their bad behavior, you have to find some way to disengage emotionally, or you will hit that wall. But we want you to know that when you do hit it, there is a feeling of awakening on the other side. You'll continue on with your life and, we hope, realize that you will not be stepmom of the year, not this year or any year, and that you must not even try to be. Take care of yourself first—emotionally and physically and spiritually. Otherwise, you won't be of any good to anyone.

Think about it this way: you know when you're on a plane and the flight attendant demonstrates the proper use of oxygen masks in an emergency? You know how rule one—no matter whom you're traveling with, no matter the age and frailty of the person you're with—is to *properly adjust the oxygen mask on yourself first*, before you help someone else? There's a reason for that rule, and it's not a selfish one, per se; it's the rule for survival, yours and anyone's around you, because if you ain't breathing the oxygen under zero oxygen conditions, then you are of no help whatsoever to anyone else. Step back, pull on your oxygen mask, and reassess. Breathe. You are not alone. If you've already been through half the tough scenarios in this book, than maybe we can save you the heartbreak of the other half. Or if you are just at the beginning of your stepmom journey, we want to make sure you never find yourself asking, "Why didn't anyone ever tell me that would happen?" We're telling you. We're telling you all the things you wish you knew…before you became a stepmom.

TAKEAWAYS

- Embrace the hit. Feel the pain, and don't feel guilty

about it. Afterward, you're more likely to let go of whatever caused that pain in the first place. A weight will be lifted from your shoulders (and psyche).

- Go forward with your family plans. Don't let the ex control your life with her manipulation and game playing.
- Once in a while, put yourself in the ex's shoes. It may be an excruciatingly bad fit, but you will gain a bit of perspective.
- The bio mom always wins. You will always be Venus to her Serena Williams.
- That said, *stop caring* about who wins!
- There will *always* be a roadblock related to the ex or the stepkids. Be prepared, especially if the road has been particularly (and uncharacteristically) smooth.
- Make a plan with your partner regarding your stepkids, and stick to it.
- You don't need to know about every conversation, email exchange, text, or minute detail concerning the ex or the stepkids, especially if it doesn't affect you. Let it go.
- You can't slay the dragon (well, maybe once in a blue moon, you will). Best to avoid her.

Afterword

"Life is a journey, not a destination."

—Anonymous

IN OUR COLLECTIVE STEPMOTHERING JOURNEYS, WE LEARNED a lot about ourselves—as mothers, parents, partners, and women—and we learned even more in the writing of this book. Ultimately, the one constant we found among ourselves and 99 percent of the stepmoms we know (and believe me, we stepmoms seem to find one another like moths to a flame) was that we are all innately nurturers. We've all inherently felt the need to protect and advocate for our stepkids and to strive to be the one constant in *their* lives. After all is said and done (and broken and thrown), regardless of all the back and forth with courts, bio moms, therapists, judges, teachers, coaches, grandparents, aunts, and uncles, *we* stepmoms are the ones who have raised the kids (our partner's *and* our own), and the frustrating irony is that everyone else— your partner, the ex, the therapist, the court-appointed judge, the coach, etc.—has had a greater voice in dictating the parameters of our stepmom lives than we have had.

As stepmoms, we've found ourselves too far down on the totem pole of "those whose voices matter." Despite the fact that we are raising our stepkids, wiping their butts, dropping them off at school, going to all their games and recitals, and bending over backward to be there for them, we generally have been given less input than anyone else in their lives. We've felt invisible to those other decision makers, despite all we've done and continue to do. We've questioned whether to remain in marriages. We've struggled to articulate our feelings and our angst, and we've been diminished in our efforts to accommodate everyone else's needs.

Would we have done it all over again? Would we have married our husbands and taken on the role of stepmom to their children if we'd known what lay ahead? That's a tough one—after all, we must be remaining anonymous for a reason, right? So seriously, would we? "Of course!" is the right answer, but it's not that simple. Sure, we're all finally on the other side (mostly) of the stepmothering vortex, and as with childbirth, the initial pain tends to dim over the years, but if we'd only had an idea of what life would be as a stepmom, if only we'd had a few tools going into this gig, we could have been *prepared* and maybe even have avoided the worst of it.

No one, not your therapist, your mother, or your best friend—and not even any of us—can tell you whether you should embark on a relationship with someone who has kids. Certainly no one would have been able to convince any of us *not* to get involved with the partners we ultimately married. (Ha! We would have dared you to try, and then we would have chewed you up and spit you out.) When you're in the throes of (or considering) a new romantic relationship with someone who has kids, you don't think of asking yourself, "Gee, I wonder what kind of relationship my boy/girlfriend and their ex have as *co-parents* of their seemingly adorable twin middle schoolers?" Obviously, we didn't.

As savvy as we imagined we were in most other aspects of our lives, we didn't think to ask any of the right questions before we jumped into our roles as stepmoms. We were naive enough to think that because we'd fallen in love with our partners, love would keep the whole carriage together! Yes, love may triumph, but it doesn't hurt to have the tools and knowledge necessary for stepmothering in this day and age. Since we've been there, done that, having run and stumbled through years of being stepmoms, we hope we've been able to clue you in on what to expect and to give you the intel to handle whatever step situation you find yourself in.

This is it, your tool guide, rule, and reference book, everything that we lived and learned. We didn't set out to make your life as a stepmom easier or happier; it just happened that way.

Live and learn. We hope that we've helped you to do both.

With love,

The Stepmoms' Club

Online Divorce
Resource Guide

The following resources and any legal discussion in this book do not comprise legal advice. The reader is responsible for seeking his or her own legal advice as appropriate for the situation and region.

American Bar Association—Family Law
https://www.americanbar.org/groups/family_law/resources.html
- FAQs about family law, supplemented by a glossary of legal terms.
- Links to the American Bar Association's guide to finding a lawyer and supplemental resources such as client manuals and state family law charts.

American Academy of Matrimonial Lawyers—Find a Lawyer
http://www.aaml.org/find-a-lawyer
- Searchable directory of attorneys specializing in matrimonial law.

Internal Revenue Service—Tax Effects of Divorce or Separation
https://www.irs.gov/uac/tax-effects-of-divorce-or-separation
- Basic explanation of the tax effects resulting from divorce or separation, including information about the impact of

child support, alimony, spousal IRA, and name changes on filing taxes.

- Information about health care law considerations in the event that there is a change in circumstance due to divorce/separation.

International Academy of Family Lawyers— Find a Lawyer
https://www.iafl.com/
- Searchable worldwide directory of attorneys specializing in family law.

Women's Law
http://www.womenslaw.org/
- Legal information and support for victims of domestic violence and sexual assault.

HG Legal Resources—U.S. Divorce Law Center
https://www.hg.org/divorce-law-center.html
- Listings of individual state divorce laws.
- Informational pages on divorce-related topics, including the fundamentals of divorce law, grounds for divorce/dissolution, annulment law, property division, alimony/spousal support, and child custody law.

Divorce Legal Resources by State
According to the most recent data (2015) compiled by the CDC, the national rate of divorce per one thousand people is 3.1 percent. States marked with an asterisk (*) have the top ten highest divorce rates according to current numbers. Link to divorce rates, by states: https://www.cdc.gov/nchs/data/dvs/state_divorce_rates_90_95_99-15.pdf.

Alabama

Alabama Legal Help—Divorce
http://www.alabamalegalhelp.org/issues/families-and-children/divorce
- Articles on the legal aspects of divorce, common questions and answers about divorce, family mediation, and postdivorce issues, and how general divorce proceedings work. Applicable only to the state of Alabama.

Alaska

Alaska Court System—Self-Help Center: Family Law
http://www.courts.alaska.gov/shc/family/selfhelp.htm
- Informational pages and videos about family law issues including divorce/dissolution of marriage, child support, family law videos, and property and debt. Applicable only to the state of Alaska.

Arizona

Arizona Court Help—Divorce Information
http://azcourthelp.org/browse-by-topic/divorce
- Printable guide to filing for divorce and a link to the Arizona Judicial Branch's page on child support and family law. Applicable only to the state of Arizona.

Arkansas

Arkansas Legal Services—Divorce Help
http://www.arlegalservices.org/node/117/divorce-help
- Fact sheets, interactive forms, and videos about annulment, divorce, and separation laws in Arkansas. Applicable only to the state of Arkansas.

California

The Judicial Branch of California—Divorce or Separation
http://www.courts.ca.gov/selfhelp-divorce.htm
- Articles discussing the basics of divorce/separation, how to file for divorce, responding to and completing a divorce/separation, spousal/partner support, property and debt in divorce/separation, and other related topics, as well as legal forms and divorce FAQs. Applicable only to the state of California.

Colorado

Colorado Judicial Branch—Divorce, Family Matters, Civil Unions
**https://www.courts.state.co.us/Forms/SubCategory.cfm?
Category=Divorce**
- Information on divorce law, family law, and partner/civil unions—all with extensive subcategories. Applicable only to the state of Colorado.

Connecticut

Connecticut Judicial Branch—Law Libraries
https://www.jud.ct.gov/lawlib/law/divorce.htm
- Variety of research manuals and articles, including FAQs, do-it-yourself divorce guides, and guides to filing and navigating a divorce. Applicable only to the state of Connecticut.

Delaware

Delaware Courts—Divorce/Annulment Overview
http://courts.delaware.gov/family/divorce/
- Overview of the divorce and annulment processes in Delaware, along with FAQs and contact information for courthouses. Also includes links to forms, instructional packets, records access, and parental guides to family court. Applicable only to the state of Delaware.

District of Columbia

District of Columbia Courts—Divorce Matters
https://www.dccourts.gov/services/divorce-matters
- Overview on filing for divorce or legal separation and information outlining grounds for separation. Applicable only to the District of Columbia.

Florida

Florida Courts—Family Law & Self Help Information
http://www.flcourts.org/resources-and-services/family-courts/family-law-self-help-information/
- Self-help resources including pages on lawyer referral, information for elders, legal aid, family law forms, alimony, visitation, child custody, domestic violence, name change, parenting plans, small claims, and dissolution of marriage. Applicable only to the state of Florida.

Georgia

State of Georgia—Divorce
https://georgia.gov/popular-topic/filing-divorce
- Basic information on what an individual looking to divorce should know, as well as a brief FAQ section. Applicable only to the state of Georgia.

Hawaii

Hawaii State Judiciary—Divorce
http://www.courts.state.hi.us/self-help/divorce/divorce
- Self-help index for individuals looking for basic information about divorce, such as divorce forms, case records, and links to other resources including licensed attorneys. Applicable only to the state of Hawaii.

Idaho

State of Idaho Judicial Branch Court Assistance Office—Forms:
Family Related
https://courtselfhelp.idaho.gov/family-related
- Forms and instructions related to family law. Applicable only
  to the state of Idaho.

Illinois

Illinois Legal Aid Online—Getting a Divorce
https://www.illinoislegalaid.org/legal-information/getting-divorce
- Information on the divorce process in Illinois, including articles
  on the cost of divorce and getting a divorce with children,
  and programs to help fill out forms to prepare for divorce.
  Applicable only to the state of Illinois.

Indiana

Indiana Judicial Branch—Divorce Forms
https://secure.in.gov/judiciary/selfservice/2486.htm
- Form packets for four categories: divorce with children (with
  or without agreement on all issues), divorce without children
  (with or without agreement on all issues). Applicable only to
  the state of Indiana.

Iowa

Iowa Judicial Branch—Divorce/Family Law Forms
**http://www.iowacourts.gov/For_the_Public/Representing_
Yourself_in_Court/DivorceFamily_Law/Forms/index.asp**
- Guides and forms for individuals seeking a divorce as well as
  information about divorce and family law. Applicable only to
  the state of Iowa.

Kansas

Kansas Legal Services—All About Kansas Divorce
http://www.kansaslegalservices.org/node/1237/all-about-kansas-divorce
- Basic information about divorce as well as applicable legal forms and a guide to finding legal help. Applicable only to the state of Kansas.

Kentucky

Legal Aid Network of Kentucky—Self-Help Divorce Options for Kentucky Residents
http://kyjustice.org/divorceforms
- Self-help informational packets and forms for filing divorce. Applicable only to the state of Kentucky.

Louisiana

Louisiana State Bar—Divorce
http://files.lsba.org/documents/PublicResources/LSBADivorce Brochure.pdf
- Brochure with general information about divorce in Louisiana, including details about property rights, spousal support, procedures, costs, and child support. Applicable only to the state of Louisiana.

Maine

State of Maine Judicial Branch—Divorce
http://www.courts.maine.gov/maine_courts/family/divorce/index.html
- Divorce forms for couples with and without children and instructions on filling out the forms, along with information about legal aid and mediation. Applicable only to the state of Maine.

Maryland

Maryland Courts—Department of Juvenile and Family Services: Family Law Forms Index
http://mdcourts.gov/family/formsindex.html
- Index of family law forms pertaining to child support, custody, divorce, financial forms, change of name forms, miscellaneous forms, and protective order and peace order forms. Applicable only to the state of Maryland.

Massachusetts

Massachusetts Court System—Divorce
http://www.mass.gov/courts/selfhelp/family/divorce.html
- Informational overview on divorce with links to articles about filing for divorce and the divorce process. Also provides information about the Family Court Answer Center as a further resource for those seeking answers on divorce and family law matters. Applicable only to the state of Massachusetts.

Michigan

Michigan Legal Help—Family
https://michiganlegalhelp.org/self-help-tools/family
- Index of articles discussing situational aspects of divorce, custody, child support, and the process of divorce. Applicable only to the state of Michigan.

Minnesota

Minnesota Judicial Branch—Divorce/Dissolution
http://mncourts.gov/Help-Topics/Divorce.aspx
- Overview on divorce, property as related to divorce, divorce forms, rules and laws, tools and resources, videos, and related legal topics. Applicable only to the state of Minnesota.

Mississippi

Mississippi Legal Services—Divorce
http://www.mslegalservices.org/resource/divorce-3
- Information and links on divorce regarding court processes, child custody, property, and assets. Applicable only to the state of Mississippi.

Missouri

Official Missouri State Website—Marriage & Divorce
https://www.mo.gov/home-family/marriage-divorce
- Information on marriage and divorce laws as well as links to divorce forms and contact information for local courts. Applicable only to the state of Missouri.

Montana

Montana Judicial Branch—Ending Your Marriage
http://courts.mt.gov/library/topic/end_marriage
- Forms for divorce/dissolution, legal separation, and annulment, as well as a questionnaire to determine what forms an individual may need to file for divorce. Applicable only to the state of Montana.

Nebraska

State of Nebraska Judicial Branch—Families & Children
https://supremecourt.nebraska.gov/self-help/families-children
- Instructions and forms pertaining to various situations of divorce and child support. Applicable only to the state of Nebraska.

Nevada

Supreme Court of Nevada—Standardized Divorce Forms
http://nvcourts.gov/Law_Library/Resources/Forms/Standardized_Divorce_Forms/
*   Divorce forms and civil cover sheet. Applicable only to the state of Nevada.

New Hampshire

New Hampshire Judicial Branch—Circuit Court Family Division, Forms
http://www.courts.state.nh.us/fdpp/forms/index.htm
*   Forms related to family law including divorce, parenting, mediation, guardianship, and name change. Applicable only to the state of New Hampshire.

New Jersey

New Jersey Courts—Self-Help Resource Center
https://www.judiciary.state.nj.us/selfhelp/index.html
*   Resource center for representing oneself in court with links to family division law including divorce, child custody, and child support. Applicable only to the state of New Jersey.

New Mexico

New Mexico Courts—Divorce
https://www.nmcourts.gov/Self-Help/divorce.aspx
*   Instructions and forms relating to divorce and family matters. Applicable only to the state of New Mexico.

New York

New York Courts—Divorce Resources
http://www.nycourts.gov/divorce/index.shtml
- Divorce resources for the state of New York including legal resources for unrepresented litigants, information on finding a lawyer, divorce FAQs, divorce by county, divorce forms and instructions, child support tools, resources for judges and attorneys, and supreme court contact information. Applicable only to the state of New York.

North Carolina

The North Carolina Court System—Frequently Asked Questions
http://www.nccourts.org/Support/FAQs/FAQs.asp?Type=14
- FAQs pertaining to separation/divorce in relation to court proceedings, financial settlement, and child support. Applicable only to the state of North Carolina.

North Dakota

North Dakota Court System—Legal Self Help Center—
Family Law
http://www.ndcourts.gov/ndlshc/FamilyLaw/FamilyLaw.aspx
- Family law information and research guides as well as links to divorce forms for various categories of divorce. Applicable only to the state of North Dakota.

Ohio

The Supreme Court of Ohio & the Ohio Judicial System—Domestic Relations and Juvenile Standardized Forms
http://www.supremecourt.ohio.gov/JCS/CFC/DRForms/
* Basic overview of forms relating to domestic relations and juveniles including divorce, parenting, and separation agreements. Applicable only to the state of Ohio.

Oklahoma

Oklahoma Bar Association—Is Divorce the Answer for You?
http://www.okbar.org/public/Brochures/divorce.aspx
* Information on grounds for divorce, power of divorce court over cases, and the process of getting a divorce, as well as an extensive Q&A about the divorce process and divorce laws. Applicable only to the state of Oklahoma.

Oregon

Oregon State Bar—Divorce in Oregon
https://www.osbar.org/public/legalinfo/1132_Divorce.htm
* FAQs discussing divorce in Oregon, including details about divorce proceedings, the necessity of having a lawyer, serving and responding to divorce papers, and the cost of divorce. Applicable only to the state of Oregon.

Pennsylvania

The Unified Judicial System of Pennsylvania—Divorce Proceedings
http://www.pacourts.us/learn/representing-yourself/divorce-proceedings
* Forms and information on representing oneself during divorce proceedings, as well as general information about the procedures of divorce. Applicable only to the state of Pennsylvania.

Rhode Island

Rhode Island Judiciary—Family Court
https://www.courts.ri.gov/Courts/FamilyCourt/Pages/default.aspx
- Information about family court, including contact information, forms, and details on the mediation program. Applicable only to the state of Rhode Island.

South Carolina

South Carolina Judicial Department—Self-Represented Litigant Simple Divorce Packets
http://www.sccourts.org/forms/indexsrldivorcepacket.cfm
- Free, interactive program to help fill out divorce packets. Applicable only to the state of South Carolina.

South Dakota

South Dakota Unified Judicial System—Divorce for the Self-Represented Litigant
http://ujs.sd.gov/Forms/divorce.aspx
- General divorce information and forms pertaining to all aspects of the divorce process. Applicable only to the state of South Dakota.

Tennessee

Tennessee State Courts—Court-Approved Divorce Forms
https://www.tncourts.gov/help-center/court-approved-divorce-forms
- Divorce forms with instructions, available in English, Spanish, and Chinese. Applicable only to the state of Tennessee.

Texas

Texas Law Help—Family, Divorce, and Children
**http://texaslawhelp.org/issues/family-law-and-domestic-violence/
divorce-free-forms?channel=legal%2Dresources**
- Fact sheets and divorce forms with instructions, many available in multiple languages, including English and Spanish. Applicable only to the state of Texas.

Utah

Utah Courts—Divorce
https://www.utcourts.gov/howto/divorce/
- Information on divorce including articles on finding an attorney, filing for divorce, the divorce process, postdivorce, and divorce education for children. Also includes a link to the Online Court Assistance Page to fill out legal forms. Applicable only to the state of Utah.

Vermont

Vermont Judiciary—Divorce
https://www.vermontjudiciary.org/family/divorce
- Information on divorce including an overview video, FAQs, and legal forms. Applicable only to the state of Vermont.

Virginia

Virginia Access to Justice Commission—Divorce
http://selfhelp.vacourts.gov/node/8/divorce
- FAQs on divorce and links to Virginia Legal Aid and Virginia State Bar information on family law and divorce. Applicable only to the state of Virginia.

Washington

Washington Courts—Court Forms: Divorce (Dissolution)
http://www.courts.wa.gov/forms/?fa=forms.contribute&formid=13
- General information and instructions for forms pertaining to divorce, as well as links to information and instructions about ending marriage from Washington Legal Help. Applicable only to the state of Washington.

West Virginia

West Virginia Judiciary—Divorce Packet Forms
http://www.courtswv.gov/lower-courts/divorce-forms/index-divorce-forms.html
- Petitioner packets, respondent packets, and parenting plan items. Applicable only to the state of West Virginia.

Wisconsin

Wisconsin Court System—Divorce and Family Law
https://www.wicourts.gov/services/public/selfhelp/divorce.htm
- Forms, resources, and procedures regarding divorce and family law. Applicable only to the state of Wisconsin.

Wyoming

Wyoming Judicial Branch—Court Self-Help Forms: Family Law
http://www.courts.state.wy.us/LegalHelp/Forms
- Family law forms with instructions regarding divorce, child support, custody, and miscellaneous family matters. Applicable only to the state of Wyoming.

Online Child Support/Blended Family Resources

American Psychological Association—Marriage and Divorce
http://www.apa.org/topics/divorce/index.aspx
- Links to articles published by the American Psychological Association relating to marriage, divorce, and blended families.
- Searchable directory of psychologists in the United States.

Office of Child Support Enforcement—Parents
https://www.acf.hhs.gov/css/parents
- Directory of state, local, and tribal child support offices.
- Printable Child Support Handbook.
- Glossary of common child support terms.
- Printable Handbook for Military Families.
- Links to other resources such as FAQs and articles on obtaining and changing child support and the federal tax refund offset program.

Child Support Tools
https://childsupporttools.com/
- Tools to calculate an estimate of child support to help individuals represent themselves in court. The reports created are required by Kansas, Missouri, and Texas Supreme Courts and are instantly recognized by courts in those states.

The Stepfamily Foundation
http://www.stepfamily.org/
- Counseling for the stepfamily/blended family, divorce counseling, remarriage counseling, and stepfamily certification seminars.
- Worldwide directory of coaches and counselors.

National Stepfamily Resource Center—Support Groups
http://www.stepfamilies.info/support-groups.php
- Directory of local chapters of the former Stepfamily Association of America that provide essential support and education to co-parents.

Index

Acknowledgments

There are so many special people who have been supportive of this book and us personally over the years.

With gratitude, this book is dedicated to those who have been an inspiration.

Family members, friends, spouses and fellow stepmoms who have provided encouragement and strength along the way to make *The Stepmoms' Club* possible, we are truly grateful.

With deep appreciation, thank you to an amazing agent and friend, Andrea "Andy" Barzvi, for believing in this project from the very beginning and for our countless conversations, your guidance, and your passion for this book.

To Karen Rizzo, for her patience, humor, and creative writing; without you this book could not have come to fruition. Thank you from the bottom of our hearts.

Thank you to our editor, Shana Drehs, and the entire wonderful team at Sourcebooks; Lathea Williams, Cassie Gutman,

Adrienne Krogh, Heather Morris, and Margaret Johnston, for their publishing expertise.

Claire Greenspan Bamundo and Greenspan Creative Marketing, we appreciate and thank you for your focus and energy to deliver a comprehensive and collaborative dynamic brand book campaign.

We wish to acknowledge and thank the attorneys and personnel at Reavis Page Jump LLP., for their time and contributions to this undertaking. In particular, we thank Heidi Reavis, Isabella Kendrick and Francesca Rizzo for their contributions to the legal discussion in this book as well as the Online Divorce Resource Guide included to assist our readers.

This book is devoted to all the stepmoms out there who have invested unwavering time, care, and love to their stepchild(ren). Welcome to our club!

About the Authors

In this book, names (ours included) have been changed in an attempt to, well, not so much protect the innocent as keep the peace. To those people who did not and would not want to be identified—including family, friends, stepkids, stepmoms, stepdads, bio moms, the brave, the stupid, the inspirational, the reckless, the stubborn, the outrageous, and the beloved—we say thank you. There would be no Stepmoms' Club without any of you.

Stephanie Block lives in Florida, where she takes long walks on the beach. After a successful career as an entrepreneur—during which time she was fortunate enough to volunteer for several nonprofits, travel, and collect jewelry and art—she sold her company and is currently blogging and managing an Etsy vintage store. Her stepmom friends continue to be her lifeline, so she plans to give every new stepmom she meets a copy of this book.

Elizabeth Ann Garrett resides in a mountainous region of the Pacific Northwest where she juggles her family and full-time career with her pursuits as an avid outdoorswoman. When there's time left over, she follows her passion for baking and cooking.

Having been in the financial industry for more than twenty-five years, **Amber Joynes** is now pursuing a career in real estate. Things she loves: her family, her girlfriends, boating, traveling, and volunteering with children's charities. She is so grateful to be able to share her experiences as a stepmom in order to help other women in the same boat. Her stepmom mantra: Have faith!

Kendall Rose has had a longtime career as a business executive in the financial services industry. She and her family reside in the Midwest, where she is also able to follow her passion for horseback riding and her volunteer work in equine-assisted therapy. Kendall can't wait for fellow stepmoms to benefit from the publication of this book.